What readers are say

Just Tell the Truth: Questions Families Ask When Gay Married Men Come Out

"The clearest and most honest answers to the questions families ask ... available. It has the unmistakable resonance of authentic experience. I am particularly impressed by the theological integrity that is integral to Dr. Norman's analysis and writing. It provides an essential and often neglected source of insight."

Dr. E. Dale Dunlap, Dean Emeritus
Saint Paul School of Theology
Kansas City, Mo.

"A very personal story. I like the straight forward approach. Dr. Norman uses short chapters and spares us charts, graphs, or other appeals to authority. ... As a personal testimony, it will draw people ... and encourage them to live out their story."

Paul Anderson, Ph.D.
Licensed Psychologist

"The story is really told in the book and in the most clear, profound way, as if Dr. Norman was telling me in person. The sentences leapt to life and the story played before me as if it were being shown on a movie screen. The spirituality interlaced throughout the entire story kept me grounded. ... The conclusion of the book leaves you not with an ending, but a sense of beginnings and optimisms."

Virginia Vaughan
A neighborhood friend

Just Tell the Truth

Questions Families Ask
When Gay Married Men Come Out

Terry Norman

Just Tell the Truth

Questions Families Ask
When Gay Married Men Come Out

By

Dr. Terry L. Norman

𝕇

PREHENSION PUBLICATIONS
Kansas City, Missouri

Just Tell the Truth: Questions Families Ask
When Gay Married Men Come Out

Copyright © 1998 by Terry L. Norman, D.Min., LPC

Published in the United States of America
by Prehension Publications, Kansas City,
and distributed internationally by the Norman Institute.

Address inquiries to: P.O. Box 45600, Kansas City, Missouri, 64171
www.NormanInstitute.org

Quotations from *Gay, Straight, and In-Between: The Sexology of Erotic Orientation* by John Money. Copyright © 1988 by Oxford University Press, Inc. Used by permission of Oxford University Press, Inc.

Limited Edition, May 1998

ISBN 0-9664796-0-2

Dedication

This book is dedicated to my children,
David, Annika and *Thomas*,
and to their mother, *Mary*.

Acknowledgments

You are going to find this a very personal book. While it is not an autobiography as such, I use my own life story throughout to illustrate the psychodynamics that motivate gay men to enter heterosexual marriage and behave the ways we do. Such an account would not have been possible without the cooperation of my own children. So I will begin by thanking them—David, Annika, and Thomas Norman. Not only have they cooperated; they have encouraged me to tell the Norman family story. I also want to thank their mother, Mary, for her remarkable willingness to see this book in print. In her own way she too has encouraged the process, and for that I am thankful. It is with good reason that I have dedicated this book to my three children and their mother.

I also wish to thank a large number of persons who must remain nameless—my clients over the past two decades, especially the gay married men, their wives and families with whom I have worked increasingly since 1990. Without them the insights and theory that unfold in the following pages would not have been possible.

I also wish to express deep gratitude for the guidance of two of my professional mentors at Saint Paul School of Theology: Dr. E. Dale Dunlap, Dean Emeritus, and Dr. Tex Sample, Professor of Church and

Society. They have shepherded my evolutionary process for over three decades. Moreover, they have provided advice and encouragement as this book unfolded, and Dr. Sample has been kind enough to write the preface.

There are four personal friends without whom this book would never have come into being, and I thank them for their love and encouragement. Charlene Ward was the first straight female in whom I confided my orientational confusion. Her acceptance and love of my gay soul have been a sustaining reality for over thirty years. Bob and Sharron Cook, friends since 1971, were the first persons who encouraged me to write the story you are about to read. They stood by me through excruciating pain as I relived the events of that story. Time and again they called me to accountability and constantly insisted that I just tell the truth. I doubt though, that the truth would ever have taken written form had a man named Calvin Williford not entered my life in 1992. It was Calvin with whom I met weekly for over two years as the pages that make up Part One gradually evolved.

I wish to acknowledge my two most important mentors in mental health counseling, Drs. Elmer Jackson and Grace Miller, by whose side I worked daily during a decade of general practice in Jefferson City. Also, I acknowledge with thanks my present colleague in professional practice, Megan Monroe, for her willingness to review and discuss the theories which gradually evolved as this book took form. And certainly, thanks goes to my friend Dr. John Lester for his insight into evolutionary psychology as it relates to gay married men.

Next, I wish to acknowledge those who helped bring the book into final form. My thanks go to the Board of Directors of the Norman Institute, all of whom read the manuscript and made many helpful suggestions, and especially to the Institute's Executive Director, Eddie Miller.

Also, I wish to offer special thanks to Pola Firestone of BookWorks for her guidance and counsel. Without Pola, the self-publication of a quality book would never have been possible. Special thanks also go to Doug Coonrod for cover design; to Van Buckley for his expertise in preparing the manuscript for publication; and to Rene Kammeier and her colleagues for actually printing the book. And finally, very special thanks goes to my editor and close personal friend, Constance Wise, for her endless hours of conversation and sensitive editing style.

I wish there were a way to acknowledge by name the many other persons who have supported me daily the past five years. No one is more representative of that group than the management and wait staff at the Classic Cup Cafe across from my office on the Country Club Plaza in Kansas City. I thank them for their patience during the countless hours at table #24, the endless cups of coffee, and their gracious words of encouragement.

Table of Contents

Preface, by Dr. Tex Sample   1

Introduction   3

Part One:
The Journey Toward Authenticity

1   When I Was Six ...   7

2   Your Quest for Truth   29

Part Two:
Questions Families Ask
When Gay Married Men Come Out

3   What is Sexual Orientation?   37

4   Is Orientation a Choice?   41

5   What Determines Orientation?   45

6   Is Same Gender Orientation a   47
    Mental Disorder?

7   Is Same Gender Orientation a   49
    Spiritual Disorder?

8   Can Orientation be Changed?   57

9   Does Orientation Determine   63
    Sexual Behavior?

10 What is Homophobia?   65

11 *How Does Internalized Homophobia*   69
Affect Gay Men?

12 *Why Do Gay Men Enter Heterosexual*   77
Marriages?

13 *Why Do Gay Men Allow Themselves*   81
to Become Fathers?

14 *When Do Gay Men Typically*   85
Discover Their True Orientation?

15 *What Happens After Discovery Occurs?*   89

16 *Why Do Some Married Men*   97
Fake Straight After Discovery of Their
Gay Orientation?

17 *How Could I Have Been So Naive?*   101

18 *What is Voluntary Disclosure, and What*   105
Motivates the Disclosure Process?

19 *What Possible Good Can Come from*   119
Voluntary Disclosure?

Conclusion   141

Appendix A: 149
On Orientational Repression

Appendix B: 153
On Polymorphous Pansexuality
and the Gay Married Male

Appendix C: 157
On Spirituality, and the Evolution
of Orientational Authenticity

Notes   163

Preface

The way we as heterosexuals deal with gay men and lesbians in a homophobic society is to use abstractions to demean and stereotype them. If we can fill our images of them with sufficient labels and distortions, we never have to address the lived reality of their lives.

It will be difficult to do this with the poignant narrative told by Terry Norman. His personal, candid, and touching story is one that needs to be heard widely in a society used to getting its information from bigoted stereotypes, from desperate souls who come to public attention as a result of arrests, and from the headline-hunting character of so much of the media.

I have known Terry for thirty years, and the beauty of this book is how much of his own life and personality come through these pages. His honesty, his sharing of the pain and doubt that have plagued his life, his courage, his sense of the suffering of others, especially those closest to him, his strength to carry on: these things among others, give his story a heart-touching quality that breaks through the heterosexism of our culture and brings us to the flesh and blood reality of a host of people in our society who live as excluded others even in the midst of the many.

Those of us with a heterosexual orientation are offered here an inside view of a good human being who loves his former wife and children and who also cannot live a lie. One is given the privilege of witnessing the struggle of a successful, gay married man with children who at mid-life faces the powerful claim of an authentic identity. Families with gay and lesbian members will find here the opportunity for deepening their sensitivity to those they love and will find answers to the many everyday questions they ask.

Homosexual men will find here, doubtlessly, much to identify with as Terry traces the turns of his own life. As a psychotherapist, he has spent thousands of hours with hundreds of gay men and their families. The book offers the wisdom wrought from long hours of listening to and working with those hammering out a way to live an honest life with families they still love and with committed partners in a heterosexist world.

It is also a spiritual journey. It entails the growing realization on Terry's part that the push and the pull of his life toward naming, claiming and living authentically as a gay man is the work of God. His discovery that God loves him, accepts him, and indeed, leads him into a loving relationship with a committed partner is a story too seldom told. His faithful search for God and God's will in his life is one of devotion and of hope.

Tex Sample, Ph.D.
Professor of Church and Society
Saint Paul School of Theology
Kansas City, Missouri

Introduction

This book is about the thousands of gay men in America who enter heterosexual marriages, father children, and remain quietly in the closet until the day they voluntarily disclose their true gender orientation. Its purpose is to provide clear, concise answers to the questions families ask when gay married men come out. If you are an individual seeking to understand the feelings and motivations of such a man, I encourage you to read on.

As I write these words my mind goes back to my own wife and three children. I remember all too well the pain and confusion they expressed when I publicly disclosed my gay orientation during the fall of 1990. I remember their questions, their many, many questions, but most of all I remember the fear and anger in their eyes.

Who wouldn't have been angry? For decades I had hidden the truth so skillfully that my family had little idea of my actual feelings. We had lived in the same community of 50,000 for over twenty years. I earned a lucrative income from private practice as a licensed mental health professional. Moreover, I was an ordained United Methodist minister with a doctorate in pastoral psychology, and was actually serving as president of the Ministerial Alliance at the time of my disclosure. Time and again my family and friends asked, "How can you possibly be gay?"

Yes, I understood their feelings of deception and betrayal. It was obvious why they wondered if I could ever be trusted again. Had the circumstances been reversed, I would have undoubtedly felt the same way. The facts remained unaltered, however; I was a gay man faking straight, and the time for full disclosure had come.

Disclosure! The term itself strikes terror in the hearts of gay married men and their families alike. It strikes terror in my heart as I disclose in the chapters that follow those things I feel you should know about Terry Norman. The uncertainty and fear associated with coming out to others never quite seems to go away. I worry about how honest I'll be able to be. Moreover, what will others think and say? Who will be helped and who will be hurt? Where will it all lead? And most importantly, what impact will disclosure in print have on the family I still love?

If you are going to read this book, however, to think its thoughts and seriously consider its ideas, then you have every right to know something about its author. I suppose that means we should start at the beginning, with a brief account of my own journey from childhood to the present.

Part One

The Journey Toward Authenticity

1

When I was Six ...

I was six years old the night I hid outside the kitchen door, straining to hear what my parents were saying. The words they used to describe my friend's father were unfamiliar, but I certainly got the general idea. He had been arrested for something sexual involving another man. He "liked men," they said. And so did I! He "didn't deserve to live," they said; so I felt I probably didn't either. After all, they were my parents, good God-fearing Southern Methodists. Who was I to question their wisdom? The next day I was forbidden ever to go to my friend's house again. I didn't.

Strange, I remember few if any names from those early childhood years. Yet, I remember the name of my friend's father, both first and last. I remember what he looked like, how he talked, and I have vivid recall of the small restaurant he owned and operated. We had eaten there often, but never again after that night. Danny's dad was an outcast.

I assume that was my first exposure to a gay married man. It was certainly my first attitude-forming experience. I learned well and quickly: it was not acceptable to have feelings for persons of one's own gender. I was horrified, afraid someone would learn my secret, afraid they would discover that I too had such feelings.

What I heard outside that kitchen door branded itself into my memory as nothing else ever had. From that day on, I continued to listen to see what else the world had to say about persons with feelings like mine. Perhaps I was hypersensitive during the years of childhood and early adolescence, but it seems there was always a lot to hear concerning what I later learned to call "sexual orientation."

Gradually I learned that the church believed individuals like me were immoral, that the doctors of mental health considered us sick, and that the law viewed any expression of same-sex behavior as criminal. It doesn't take a doctorate in psychology to understand what a devastating impact all that had on my emotional development and sense of self-esteem.

In retrospect it seems clear that I began struggling with the issue of orientation in early childhood, long before I had either the vocabulary or cognitive ability to understand what it all meant. Somehow I knew at a visceral level that I was both emotionally and physically attracted to persons of my own gender. Even at six years of age.

At first the shame and guilt I experienced were based on inner feelings alone, but as the years of childhood passed my behavior provided ample evidence that I was right about myself. There were the little sex games with other children—the times we played "doctor" or "house," or whatever gave us an excuse to take off our clothes. I will never forget being caught under the front porch by my mother one summer afternoon. I don't recall the details of what we were doing, but I certainly remember the humiliation and guilt I felt as she delivered her stern lecture. I also knew that lecture would have been much, much worse had she known I was interested in boys, not girls.

Apparently I learned a valuable lesson from being caught that day, because I was never caught again. I wasn't caught when I spied on my older male cousins in the bathroom. Nor was I caught when I spied on some professional wrestlers dressing in their locker room. How a nine- or ten-year-old boy gained entry to a restricted area and located an observation point without being detected is beyond my imagination. Where the courage came from to take such risk I do not know. But caught or not, I know I always came away from such events feeling all the more shame and guilt as a result of my behavior. I felt I really was a despicable person and deserved the scorn of others. I disgusted even myself.

Given such feelings and behaviors, my protective instinct dictated the only course of action: I had to hide the truth about Terry from the outside world, no matter how great the isolation. My very survival depended on the ability to fake straight until I could figure out what else to do.

I think it is fair to say that I became a master role player very early in life. Not once during childhood or adolescence was I questioned about my orientation. There were no statements, no accusations, and as far as I know, no suspicions. Apparently I exhibited none of the stereotypical traits normally associated with same gender orientation. My "fake score" was one-hundred percent, an A-plus.

I may have seemed calm and together on the outside, but on the inside I was torn apart. On one hand, I wanted desperately to be straight, to avoid looking at or thinking about other guys. On the other hand, there was magnetism about the beauty of the male form that had the power to sabotage my best intentions. I must have promised myself ten thousand times never to look again, but I always did. It was as if there were two of me, the one who was determined to be straight, and the other who would have no part of it. Indeed, I was a "union of opposites,"[1] at constant war with myself.

There are those who will read this and say that children simply don't know that much about themselves, particularly regarding underlying gender orientation. They will maintain that I "could not have known" what is reported here. I suspect such a position will only be taken by individuals who are themselves straight, who have been spared the experience of growing up gay in a heterosexually dominated society.

Seldom do I see a gay client in my counseling practice who doesn't eventually say something like "Dr. Norman, I've known I was gay since childhood; I just didn't know what to call it back then." Such a statement accurately reflects the experience of most gay men and lesbians I know. Although in childhood we lack sufficient information, vocabulary, and cognitive skills to understand our dilemma fully, emotionally we seem to suspect the truth about ourselves.

At any rate, I certainly suspected the truth about myself, and the hormonal changes of puberty only served to reinforce those suspicions. Constantly during adolescence, I found myself struggling to control both my emotions and behavior. Yes, I had some attraction to girls, but deep inside I knew I was forcing those feelings upon myself, that I really wanted to be with other young men.

As I remember it, adolescence was terrible for me, much worse than childhood had been. I held on by a string, constantly wondering what was to become of me. Yet through it all, I was elected president of the student body and selected "most likely to succeed" by my classmates. Yes, I succeeded all right—in becoming an impostor whose real identity was known to no one.

Thankfully though, those teenage years also brought a basis for real hope. It was during adolescence that I learned many young men went through a period when they felt attracted to other young men, when they feared they might be homosexual. I was told the "phase" was normally outgrown, and that most of us went on to marry and live well-adjusted heterosexual lives. Such was the collective "wisdom" of the day.

It is hard to overstate the relief I felt upon hearing that news. Maybe, just maybe, I had been making too much out of all this. Maybe I too would outgrow any interest in persons of my own gender. The mere possibility left me feeling more normal and gave a sense of hopefulness to the future. Perhaps for the first time ever, I felt truly optimistic.

But the good news didn't stop there. From sources I can no longer identify, I also learned there were doctors who understood what had gone wrong with persons like me, what had happened in our early lives that left us plagued with unnatural gay tendencies. But more important than simply understanding the cause of homosexuality, they knew how to cure it!

With that information I think I persuaded myself that everything would eventually turn out fine. I came to see myself as a heterosexual who simply had not yet achieved sufficient masculinity. If I didn't outgrow my gay tendencies naturally, I would find the right book, or the right doctor, or the right treatment program, and do whatever was necessary until I was cured. Yes, there was every reason for optimism. I could and I would be straight—it was just a matter of time and will power.

So now you know the assumptions I took into adulthood concerning myself and the nature of same gender orientation. In summary, I believed:

1. Homosexuality was a mental disorder;

2. Homosexuality resulted from environmental experiences early in life;

3. Persons who engaged in same-sex behavior were deviate and immoral;

4. Most individuals outgrew their gay tendencies with the passing of time; and

5. Treatment was available to cure those of us who didn't outgrow such tendencies.

That system of thought provided considerable comfort and guidance as I moved into the serious dating years of college and seminary. During high school, I dated a number of different girls briefly, but the whole concept of "love and marriage" took on real meaning once I learned it was the solution to my orientational confusion. I threw myself into the art of loving and had one romance that saw me through all five years of college. In fact, I became engaged and undoubtedly would have married had my fiancée been willing to become the spouse of a United Methodist minister. My departure for seminary ended that relationship, however, and with its end came relief and a new enthusiasm for life.

Only a few weeks elapsed before I met the woman who was eventually to become my wife. To this day, I have vivid recall of the first moment we looked into one another's eyes. Everything about her intrigued and fascinated me. I knew immediately this was the woman I wanted to marry—the woman who would make me totally straight! I was beside myself with excitement.

I thought of Mary constantly in the months that followed. I wanted so much to date her, but I was the newly appointed minister of youth at a local church and she was only a high school junior. Gradually though, a relationship did develop and we began dating openly during her senior year.

Following Mary's graduation, she went away to college and I remained in seminary. We continued to see one another often, however, and became engaged some two years later. From the day we met, I don't believe I really considered any other option: we would marry, raise a family, and live happily ever after. My world of the late 1960s offered no other possibility.

I don't want to give you the impression that those heterosexual dating years of college and seminary were without orientational conflict. Quite to the contrary, the conflict continued as life brought one opportunity after another for sexual experimentation with other young men. And yes, the temptation was occasionally too great, and I did act upon a number of those opportunities.

During college it always seemed to be exactly that—sexual experimentation—coupled with the need for hormonal release. But things changed dramatically in seminary when I met two different young men for whom I learned to care deeply. Suddenly, being sexual with others was about emotional fulfillment. I was scared to death! It was one thing to be sexual with another man occasionally, but it was quite another to think that I might be falling in love. Such a possibility was simply too much to bear, and I quickly withdrew completely from both relationships.

Each encounter was limited both physically and emotionally, yet each left me feeling deeply guilty and convinced that heterosexual marriage was the only natural and truly fulfilling way of life. In a sense, each experience strengthened my determination to become the person I felt I should be—a happily married heterosexual male.

Sadly, I never told my fiancée about my private battle or the role she played in the victory I envisioned. I kept all that to myself, and shortly after my graduation from seminary, we announced our wedding plans. It is hard to say who was more naive when we exchanged vows. Whatever the case, I emerged a married Elder in the United Methodist Church, confident that my gay inclinations would soon become a thing of the past.

After all, everything seemed to be going my way at last. I had a wife whom I loved, a new job as pastor of a new church, and an unwavering determination to become a well-adjusted heterosexual male. The pastorate proved to be a wonderful and successful experience, but no less so than our marriage. Mary and I got along well in spite of the frantic pace which seemed to characterize our life. Workwise, I spent most mornings in the church office, made pastoral calls in the afternoons, and then returned to the church three or four evenings per week for meetings. Merely to say that life was busy is a gross distortion of reality. We seldom had a moment to spare in those days.

Without doubt though, the births of David and Annika stand out as the high points from those early years of marriage. My wife and I both wanted children, and I shall never forget her euphoria—her complete utter joy—as she held our healthy babies for the first time. Words cannot convey the beauty I experienced in her as those precious moments unfolded. It was truly awesome to stand beside Mary's bed, knowing I had been part of making those moments become reality.

Even now I see David's huge eyes as he looked up from the incubator, wrapped in a soft white blanket. I hear Annika's first cry as she was held by the heels and slapped gently on the bottom. I was there, watching part of me come to life! No memories are more precious, no moments more sacred. Even as I write these words, tears of joy flow from my heart as I experience those miraculous events yet once again.

While the gift of physical birth was awesome, no less wonderful were the moments of emotional intimacy. I don't know Annika's age as she stood in her bed, holding its railed-side, but I shall never forget the words "I love you, Daddy," as they slipped from her little mouth for the first time.

Nor will I forget a Holiday Inn breakfast with David shortly after his fourth birthday. We often had breakfast there as I took him to nursery school each Tuesday and Thursday morning. I can still feel his little arms holding me tight as he realized that death was a part of life. He cried and shook as he realized the time would come when the father he loved would die. A few days later, David came up with the perfect solution. He simply said, "Daddy, when you have to die, we'll just die together. That way I won't have to live without you." He seemed perfectly happy with his solution, and the whole event quietly passed into memory.

I knew from the beginning that I wouldn't trade anything for fatherhood. It was wonderful, absolutely wonderful.

Needless to say, those were all busy years, and there was little opportunity to focus on my long-standing inner conflict regarding gender orientation. In retrospect, I think I basically ignored my feelings, simply pretending as if that conflict no longer existed. Yet deep inside I always knew the truth; I knew that nothing had really changed.

It is hard to say when I consciously realized that I had been systematically suppressing my emotions. One thing is clear, however: my wife recognized my depression before I did, and it was her concern and persistence that finally brought me to speak the unspeakable. That disclosure to her, my first to anyone ever, began a process that was to continue for the next fifteen years.

Ah yes, disclosure to Mary! You need to know the details. It was late summer of 1975, no more than three months after Annika's birth. It may have actually been our first evening out alone since her arrival. The restaurant, our favorite at the time, was almost empty as we sat staring across the table at one another. After four years of marriage, my wife knew something was wrong, and she was determined to know what. I'll never forget how uncomfortable I felt as she pressed for an answer.

"Are you involved with another woman?" she asked. "If you are, just tell me. Something has caused you to lose interest in our relationship, and I want to know what." To say that she was insistent is an understatement; she needed an answer and was determined that I would provide it before we left that table.

To the best of my recollection, I finally managed to say something like "No ... I'm not involved with anyone ... but if I were ... it probably wouldn't be ... a woman." I thought the world would end that moment.

But our world didn't end. Instead, we talked for hours and I explained that I had gradually come to think of myself as bisexual, admitting that I frequently had feelings for other men. I recall characterizing myself as "eighty-percent straight" and assuring her I could handle whatever history proved the other twenty percent to be. I recall saying something like, "I have no intention of allowing my interest in men to sabotage our marriage, and I could never, ever adopt a gay lifestyle."

I could not believe what I was saying even as the words came from my mouth. I had not intended to tell her anything, yet I was revealing my lifelong secret and speaking in terms of "bisexuality." Where was all this coming from? Why was I sharing it now? And most importantly, how was my wife going to respond?

The grace with which Mary handled that evening still amazes me. There were moments of intense anger, but on the whole she was compassionate and understanding, actually showing more love for me than I felt for myself. "Terry," she said, "I don't want this to destroy our marriage either. We'll take all the time you need and work this thing through together. There has to be a solution."

What I remember is a very empathic woman who reacted to my disclosure with maturity and courage. There was no condemnation, no rejection, no demands nor threats. Quite to the contrary, in fact, her love and acceptance actually seemed to increase after that night.

The immediate result was great relief for both of us. I had finally shared my deepest darkest secret with the very person from whom I most needed to hide it, and she finally had a logical explanation for my lack of emotional intimacy and tendency toward isolation. Yes, it was a good start. The ice was finally broken, and our relationship appeared to be on the road toward real authenticity.

As the weeks and months passed, we frequently reclaimed the spirit of that evening and openly discussed the dilemma posed by my orientational confusion. But there were always questions which I either couldn't or wouldn't answer, questions which required me to look more honestly at myself than I felt capable of doing. Increasingly, I responded to my wife's inquiries with hostility and again withdrew into myself. To avoid the pain, we gradually slipped into a conspiracy of silence in which my orientation simply wasn't mentioned. The very recall of the quiet years that followed leaves me with a profound sense of deep sadness.

During those years of silence, we went on to develop and enjoy "the good life" together. We loved one another and remained determined to make our marriage work. Moreover, we were determined to make Jefferson City our permanent home.

I know, I know, you're saying that clergy don't go anywhere and stay permanently. Normally that's true, but I came from a family that relocated so often that I never wanted to move again. I attended four different schools in three different towns before completing sixth grade. My actual count of different houses we occupied prior to high school graduation fades out at ten. Moving was probably the one thing my family of origin did best. It was certainly the one thing from which I intended to protect my children.

So it isn't hard to understand why we took a parsonage allowance, bought a small house, and settled in. I had every intention of actually retiring in the same community where my ministry began. I would show the world that I was a person with roots. I would not allow orientational confusion to sabotage my plans.

Eventually, Mary and I built a new home in the country for ourselves and our two children. We had two cars and a Jeep in the driveway, two horses in the pasture, and all the debt which accompanied such a lifestyle. We took long and frequent camping trips where we attempted to leave the frustrations of daily living far behind. I was admitted to a graduate program in counseling psychology, hoping the knowledge discovered there would eventually bring peace to my increasingly troubled soul.

As time passed, my brother and his wife decided to make Jefferson City their home. My parents followed, as did Mary's sister and her husband, and finally her parents. Eventually, we were all there—all ten adults and six children—sharing one another's lives, joy, and pain. From the outside, the Norman clan must have looked like the perfect all-American family.

But things were far from perfect for me on the inside. I spent those years between 1975 and the end of the decade at constant war with myself. On the one hand, I struggled to become fully the heterosexual male I so much wanted to be. I was determined to change, and read book after book on the cause and cure of homosexuality. I prayed constantly for divine intervention and even disclosed my dilemma to a few trusted friends. I hoped their understanding and acceptance would help me better understand and accept myself. On the other hand, I went through long periods of denial when I refused to deal with any issue related to gender orientation.

Well, change finally came all right, but certainly not the sort I had wanted nor anticipated. Gradually I found myself resigned to the fact that my feelings would never be any different, that I would occasionally encounter a man to whom I would be both physically and emotionally attracted. I came to believe that this was a reality with which I simply had to live.

But there was another subtle change as well. I had gained absolute confidence in my ability to control my behavior and continue faking straight as long as necessary. After all, I had made it through the first half of my life without detection. There was no reason I couldn't continue that pattern indefinitely.

Moreover, I believed that to be the only responsible course of action. So gay, straight, or in between, I would continue living a heterosexual lifestyle as long as God gave me breath. I would be true to my commitments and responsible to the people I loved, regardless of the personal sacrifices involved.

With those well-fixed convictions, I eased into my forties with more peace and self-confidence than I had ever known. Professionally, I took a newly earned master's degree in counseling psychology and established what eventually proved to be a successful private practice. But the really big news came on the family front. After many long and serious conversations, my wife and I agreed to have a third child.

It was certainly a mutual decision and I recall clearly when and where it was made. Everything seemed right that early fall afternoon as we drove Interstate 70 into St. Louis for a weekend visit with Mary's parents. We were passing mile marker 175 when I found myself saying "yes," and I knew full-well that it was one of the most conscientious decisions of my life. I knew I had changed greatly in the years since the births of David and Annika, and that I would be far more present emotionally when our third child came into the world. Yes, I felt it was the right decision at the right time. With our two children securely buckled in the back seat, we drove the remaining miles into St. Louis with the realization that eventually there would be three.

What I wasn't expecting, though, was the extent to which natural childbirth would provide the opportunity for my *physical* presence when Tom was born less than a year later. I will never forget the hot

August evening when Mary and I sat on a downtown park bench, awaiting the time to drive her the last few blocks to the hospital. But when we arrived this time, the hospital didn't banish me to the fathers' waiting area. Instead, I accompanied Tom and his mother into the delivery room. I was there, watching, as his little body gradually emerged from hers. Even now I can see the delivery room lights being lowered as Tom was placed in his first warm water bath. And never, never will I forget the feel of that water on my own hands as I gently bathed our new son! There was great sensitivity from everyone present as this new life adjusted to his new world, and I was there to experience it all.

Having Tom was great, absolutely great! He completed our family, and I left the hospital the morning following his birth fully convinced I could be both husband to Mary and father to our three children as long as I lived.

Yes, as the 1980s began, our family appeared well situated for the decades ahead. It is hard to say how long my own sense of contentment and self-confidence lasted—perhaps a couple of years. But, I do know it began to give way to new pain as I sat month after month, often twenty to thirty hours per week, listening to predominately heterosexual clients tell their stories. I was there as they courageously faced the truth about themselves. I shared in their agony, and I watched as the truth set so many of them free.

Those clients unknowingly became my teachers, each contributing something to my own evolving awareness of truth. Gradually I realized that a new quest for even greater authenticity had begun at the depth of my soul, and that I was no longer listening to the pat answers offered by others, but listening instead to my own inner voice. That was a *huge* change for me, to listen to Terry rather than those external forces which I had always allowed to control me. Little did I know how that single change would alter my life as the decade unfolded.

It is fair to say that the quest to become my own authentic self became the driving force of life. Authenticity became the sacred principle around which I gradually reorganized my very being.

No single decision contributed to that quest more dramatically than the decision to enter a seminary-based doctoral program where psychology was studied in a theological context. Upon entering that program, I had no idea what it meant to "think theologically" or "integrate theology and psychology." Those concepts were as foreign to me as the Greek I had been expected to master some fifteen years earlier. Yet here I was, once again learning from the faculty of Saint Paul School of Theology in Kansas City.

That process went on four long and wonderful years. I finally graduated in 1985 with a dissertation titled *Pastoral Psychotherapy As Ontological Reorientation—A Process Model.* I know how nonsensical that title must sound, but it simply means getting in touch with the basic nature of things . . . so we can fit into reality . . . rather than struggle against it.

This is a crucial concept, so let me illustrate with an example: A little girl sits on the floor trying to put the blocks inside a funny ball. If someone convinces her that the round blocks go through the square holes, she is in for endless hours of frustration. The process only works when she figures out that the round blocks go through round holes, the square blocks through the square holes, etc. There is a given nature to that funny ball, a given structure, and satisfaction is achieved only when she identifies and conforms to that structure.

So you are wondering what all that has to do with gender orientation and the purpose of this book? Well, it was during those years of quest at Saint Paul's when I realized I'd been trying to conform my life to a set of faulty assumptions, that I had been operating on lies rather than the truth and trying to force "round blocks through square holes."

Everything began to change as God led me to integrate my own life experience with modern psychological insight. I began to see that I was not a disordered personality as I had been led to believe, but an emotionally resilient individual who had survived a forty-year battle. Moreover, I came to realize that my gay orientation was intrinsic to my very nature, not the result of something external that had happened to me. Somehow I knew that my feelings were neither immoral nor deviant, but the result of my God-given orientation. I knew that God loved me just as I was— and I was gay. *There was nothing to outgrow, nothing which needed to be changed, and certainly nothing to cure.*

Miraculously, as I talked about ontological reorientation as the goal of the therapeutic process, I myself became reoriented. Finally, I could affirm the fact that I was one-hundred-percent, through-and-through gay. I knew that all I had told myself to the contrary had merely been an effort to conform to the expectations of others. The process had been long and tedious, but I could finally say that I knew, accepted, and loved Terry.

So now that I knew myself as the gay man I was, now that I loved and accepted myself as the very man God had created, why then did I set out systematically to destroy myself? The fact is, all my new realizations brought with them a depression more severe than any I had ever known, a depression which reached life-threatening proportions by the end of the decade. During that period, I slept more and more. I stopped exercising, ate and drank far too much, gained seventy pounds, and saw my waist size increase from 32 inches to 42 inches. Each holiday season, I looked at family photographs and saw a man who looked a little more dead than the year before. No, the years following reorientation, following the discovery of truth, were not easy for me. And I knew why.

I knew below the surface of my typically calm exterior existed a rage which I dared not fully express. How could I tell anyone that I felt victimized by life, force-fed a set of fraudulent assumptions by which I had tried to live for forty-five years? How could I possibly express the anger I felt toward myself for being so gullible for so long? I was enraged that my parents, my church, and my society had unknowingly consorted together to deny me the one and only life I had to live. But perhaps I was most enraged at myself for the dishonesty that had become part of my life, and for the way I had victimized both myself and others.

Why was I depressed? I knew the truth finally, and that truth had set my soul free from the lies which had enslaved me, yet all that internal change seemed to mean nothing in terms of my external world. I was still "the Reverend Dr. Norman," a married man with three children who earned a living as a psychotherapist in the same community where I'd lived for almost twenty years. I had the respect, love and trust of both my family and community. I felt all that would be destroyed if the truth were ever known, that my family might never recover from the shock and humiliation.

So why was I depressed? I felt trapped. I saw no way out of my dilemma in this lifetime. Responsibility required keeping my mouth shut and carrying on the charade at which I was so well practiced.

It seems, however, that all fantasy eventually comes to an end, and that no charade can go on forever. As I stepped onto the scale the morning of my forty-seventh birthday, it reflected back an astonishing two hundred-thirty pounds. That's an enormous amount of weight for a five-foot, eight-inch frame. That was New Year's Eve 1989, and I knew what my resolution for 1990 had to be. No, it wasn't to lose weight, but rather to put my external world in order. I had come to realize that I could not go on this way. I realized my very existence depended on living an authentic lifestyle, living in a way congruent with my true inner feelings. Once again, life presented me with no option; I had to disclose my true gender orientation and begin living as a fully honest person. Failure to do so meant resigning myself to premature death.

As the clouds of confusion lifted in the weeks that followed, I found myself able to admit that orientational authenticity was certainly about my need for freedom to be sexual with a person of my own gender. But far more importantly, I realized it was about the freedom to build a life with someone of my own gender: to live together in a committed relationship; to share one another's body and soul; to shop together; to cook and wash dishes together; to clean house and do laundry together; to vacation together; and yes, to dream of a future together.

Beyond all that, however, existed the most important need of all—the need for personal integrity. Gradually I realized that coming out was an act of mature self-love, that it involved breaking the bonds of shame and claiming the right to be myself. Even if I eventually took a vow of sexual celibacy, even if I never entered a committed emotional relationship with another man, I still needed to affirm myself by letting others know the real Terry. No new charade would do.

Given what I believed to be a clear choice between life and death, my decision was obvious. Month by month, the coming-out process gained momentum. By the end of 1990, I had shared the truth with everyone who I felt needed to know—my wife and children, members of my extended family, colleagues at the counseling center, my physician, my attorney, numerous close friends, and finally, my bishop.

I wish I could tell you that the transition following that disclosure was smooth and pleasant. Nothing, of course, could be further from the truth, particularly with regard to Mary and the children. I had always protected them with deception; now it seemed I was destroying them with honesty. Often I wanted to turn back, to recant my words, to pretend as if the whole nightmare had never happened.

I don't even pretend to know how badly they hurt or how many sleepless nights they had; I only know fully of my own pain. The transition was pure hell, and often I wondered if any of us would make it through intact.

Only the presence of God in our lives can account for the fact that we survived those days. The stress was unbearable, but the divine ally was always there—leading the unfolding moment into its most positive potential. I believe it was God who helped my family formulate and ask their questions. I certainly know it was God who empowered me to give straightforward, honest answers. As treacherous as the journey felt, the course always remained clear. The spirit of God spoke up from the depth of my soul, reminding me constantly that disclosure was about integrity, about removing the invisible walls of secrecy and deceit which separated me emotionally from the people I loved. Though I often wanted to turn back, I never really doubted that God had led this moment in time to become what it was. In a sense, that made going on easy, for the suffering and pain had purpose: it was the rite of passage into the peace of authenticity—with its gifts of spiritual, emotional, and physical well-being.

2

Your Quest for Truth

You now know more about the author than I've known about myself most of my life, and about the journey that brought my family and me to the authenticity which characterizes our lives today. Let us turn now to you, and to the journey that brought you to this book.

I suspect it's a safe bet that you have read this far because a married man you know has disclosed his own gay orientation sometime in your recent past. Perhaps it's a man you love—a spouse, a father, or a son to whom you gave birth decades ago. Whatever the case may be, you are most likely feeling betrayed and angry as a result of his life-shattering disclosure.

Unlike many individuals who attempt to deny the reality of such disclosure, you are seeking factual information as to why gay married men behave the ways we do. You are on a quest for truth, and it is that quest that brings you to read these very words.

Yes, I understand that you have questions and I believe they deserve honest, straightforward answers.

In all likelihood, however, the man in your life either cannot or will not provide the information you so desperately need. It is for that reason that I have undertaken the authorship of this book. I want you to have those answers, just as I wanted my family to have them at the time of my own disclosure.

Admittedly, it is a presumptuous and intimidating task to speak for other persons without their permission. Self-doubt and insecurity have persuaded me on numerous occasions to allow someone else to assume the responsibility and risk of undertaking this work. In fact, I have systematically engaged in any diversion that appeared to provide justifiable reason not to write.

To have taken pen in hand has been surrender for me. I believe most of the words which make up the chapters of this book have flowed directly from my soul onto these pages of print. But what exactly do I mean by such a statement? Before addressing the questions that pertain to your quest for truth, it seems important to make clear what I mean by the term "God."

The God of whom I speak in this book has been known by many names and understood in many ways across the course of human history. Some of us first heard of the one I call "God" within the mosque or temple. Still others heard of the creative spirit of the universe around tribal campfires as they illuminated the dark of night. I myself first heard of God within the Judaic-Christian tradition. There "he" was called Yahweh, and the people of the synagogue and church referred to their God as a "heavenly father."

In congruence with my upbringing, you will find that I frequently speak of God in the chapters which follow as if physical in form and masculine in gender. In reality, though, the process theologian in me has come to think of my higher power as pure spirit, universal in nature, and totally devoid of both physical form and gender characteristics.

Looking back, I've come to realize that my religious upbringing gave birth to a life-long spiritual quest to know God for myself, and it is from that journey inward that such conceptualizations have arisen. Once I thought I could write this book without reference to that quest, without the use of terms such as "God" or "soul" or "spirituality." But I can no more tell my life story without referring to my higher power than I can live without food or water.

I am saying that we are all spiritual beings, that we are not limited only to a physical reality. At least, that's the position you will find me systematically taking as this book unfolds. I believe, in fact, that embedded within the emotional essence of every individual is an aspect of the psyche which I have gradually come to think of as soul. I see soul as the very core of our ego, the point at which God and the individual become one in spirit. It is there, within our deepest, least-known selves, that spirituality resides and seeks to lead our lives toward authenticity.

As you will discover in both Chapter 7 and Appendix C, I have a lot more to say about the role of spirituality in the discovery and disclosure process of gay married men, and how process theology has brought illumination to what was once a dark journey. As you grapple with that material, you will begin to understand why I maintain that the journey toward orientational authenticity is inevitably a spiritual pathway, one along which the traveler finds himself or herself constantly accompanied by a God who refuses to go away.

Regardless of how you as a reader feel about my view of God, I must write this book in a way consistent with my own spiritual experience. And make no mistake about it, the book in your hands is critically needed, whether written by me now or later by some other previously married gay man. You see, the questions families ask can only be answered by someone who has himself lived the experience about which he writes.

Keep in mind, however, that I speak from the perspective of a theologically trained mental health professional who works exclusively with persons dealing with issues related to gender orientation. For better or worse, the uniqueness of such a position sets me apart from the typical gay married man, and may affect my answers in ways I do not fully recognize.

That's a risk I must take, however, and in Part Two you will find clear, straightforward answers to the questions families most often ask when a gay married man voluntarily discloses his true orientation. I have held one principle above all others in preparing these answers—to tell the truth in every word I write. After all, that is the title of the book, and you have every right to expect full candor from its author. In keeping with that principle, I have endeavored to set forth my honest conviction on each subject covered without undue regard for the opinion of others.

Yes, I know truth is often frightening, yet it literally has the power to save our lives. Truth heals individuals and sick relationships. It has the potential to displace isolation and loneliness with authentic intimacy. It liberates us from the secrets and deceptions of the past. It sets us free to embrace the potentials of the future. I believe truth adds both length and vitality to life. It is the energy, the life force of new being. My single most important goal in undertaking the authorship of this book is to persuade you to embrace the power of truth and allow it to transform your future.

§ § §

Now that we have covered my reasons for writing this book and the quest for truth that brought you to it, let's look briefly at the basic structure of Part Two itself. You will find there seventeen chapters, each addressing a different question which families tend to ask when gay married men come out.

As you work through Part Two, I believe you will begin to understand the complex psychodynamics motivating the behavior of gay married men. Throughout the text, you will find an intentional effort on my part to reflect upon my own life experience, then to theorize as to its applications to others.

And, as you will soon discover, my life experience includes extensive professional counseling with a large number of gay married men, the result of which has culminated in three hypotheses which are set forth in Appendixes A through C. I have decided to set this more clinical material aside in order not to trouble the casual reader with unnecessary theory.

I want this book to be "easy reading." Accordingly, I've made every effort to "write the way I talk." I am determined to maintain a conversational format, even if it stretches literary style to its limit.

You will also find that I have written each chapter as free-standing, yet each relates to all the others in a sequential flow. Without doubt, the theoretical cornerstone of my work will be found in the sections on homophobia and its effects on gay men. I encourage you to read this material with great care, and preferably more than once. As you grasp the concept of orientational repression, you will begin to understand why gay married men behave the ways we do.

The progressive unfolding of my own life story will, I hope, tie everything together. By the time you are finished, you should have a thorough understanding of how disclosure affected the Norman family with the passing of time. The relevance of that story to your own family, of course, is up to you to determine.

I hope you will work your way through the chapters of Part Two with a combination of open-minded acceptance and critical suspicion. I encourage you to read with pen in hand. Write in the columns and mark up the pages. (There are even blank pages left in this book for just that purpose.) Make this book yours by thinking and feeling for yourself, by reacting to its contents honestly.

And finally, as much as I hope you will find the chapters of Part Two helpful as you struggle with the questions families ask when gay married men come out, I hope even more that you will look toward your own higher power for ultimate guidance. Therein, I believe, lies our greatest source of help in any quest for truth.

Part Two

Questions Families Ask When Gay Married Men Come Out

3

What Is Sexual Orientation?

"Terry," our straight male friend asked good-naturedly, "let's assume you and Jeff have a serious auto accident on your way home tonight. Let's assume . . . oh . . that your back is broken . . . that you become permanently paralyzed. I mean, no more sex for you, ever. Now, here's the question: Are you still gay?"

Jeff and I had been a couple for almost five years, something everyone at the dinner party clearly understood. We sat speechless for a few moments, then began to answer the question together. "Of course we'd still be gay. Sex or no sex, we'd still want to live together, to share our lives, to talk about our innermost feelings, to allow ourselves to love and be loved by one another. Orientation is a matter of the heart. It goes to the very core of who we are spiritually and emotionally. How often and with whom we express ourselves sexually is only a small part of what orientation is really about."

In his 1988 publication *Gay, Straight & In-Between*, Dr. John Money of John Hopkins University reports on twenty-five years of research into the phenomenon commonly called "sexual orientation."

Surprisingly, he seldom uses the term itself. Instead, Dr. Money uses terms such as "gender orientation" and "orientational status." But the great breakthrough to my own understanding came when I experienced him as suggesting that the most appropriate term of all might actually be "homophilia."[2] That is, same-gender LOVE (from the Greek: *homo*, meaning "same" plus *philia*, meaning "love").

I am deeply indebted to Dr. Money and shall draw heavily upon his work throughout this book. Through his insights into the real nature of orientation, I have gradually come to understand that what drew Jeff and me together actually had remarkably little to do with sex itself. Rather, the power motivating our relationship has always been a deep need to love and be loved by an individual gender-appropriate to our innate, God-given orientation.

So what is "orientation"? In contemporary usage, the term attempts to describe the complex phenomenon by which we are drawn both physically and emotionally to one gender as opposed to the other. But the most important aspect to recognize is that orientation represents the direction of one's deepest need for love—toward the same gender (*homophilia*); toward the opposite gender (*heterophilia*); or toward both genders (*biphilia*). Such direction is characterized by the desire for an intimate relationship of body and mind in which two persons seek to become one, while simultaneously maintaining their own unique individuality.

The concept of orientation as gender-appropriate LOVE is relatively new in the history of western thought, yet nothing short of that very concept captures the spirit of what draws and holds two gay men together. And should their life journeys take these individuals in different directions, love has the power to transform romance into authentic friendship, thus freeing both to support one another emotionally as they move into their separate futures.

I believe it is time that our society understand mature, fully-evolved orientation for what it actually is—the desire to love and be loved by a gender-appropriate partner in a committed, on-going relationship.[3] It is time to understand that sexual expression between mature individuals—be they gay, straight, or in-between—is ultimately an act of communication. It says, "I love you, and with all that I am, I accept your love for me."

4

Is Orientation a Choice?

Stated differently, is gender orientation a matter of preference? No, not according to Dr. John Money. He states:

> A heterosexual man or woman does not become heterosexual by preference. There is no option, no plan. Becoming heterosexual is something that happens—an example of the way things are, like being tall or short, left-handed or right-handed, color-blind or color-seeing. Being homosexual is no more a preference than being heterosexual. No one, boy or girl, man or woman, prefers to be homosexual instead of heterosexual. Likewise, no one prefers to be bisexual instead of monosexual. *One either is or is not bisexual, homosexual, or heterosexual.* (Italics mine)

> Sexual preference is a moral and political term. Conceptually it implies voluntary choice, that is, that one chooses, or prefers, to be homosexual instead of heterosexual or bisexual, and vice versa. Politically, sexual preference is a dangerous term, for it implies that if homosexuals choose their preference, then they can be legally forced, under threat of punishment, to choose to be heterosexual.

> The concept of voluntary choice is as much in error here as in its application to handedness. . . .[4]

Furthermore, Dr. Money makes it clear that "falling in love" is the single most descriptive characteristic of orientation, and that we have no choice as to the gender of the individual with whom we fall in love. To quote Dr. Money directly, he sees

> falling in love as the definitive criterion of homosexual, heterosexual, and bisexual status. A person with a homosexual status is one who has the potential to fall in love *only* with someone who has the same body sex—the same genital and body morphology—as the self.[5] (Again, italics mine.)

Obviously, one of the world's most experienced research clinicians into the determinants of gender orientation has concluded that orientation is a matter of love, and that personal choice plays no role in the direction which that love takes.

Dr. Money sees "sexual preference" as both a political and a moral concept. He explains the political danger: laws which try to force persons to choose to be heterosexual. But what about the moral dimension of the concept of "sexual preference"?

In September 1997, the leaders of the Roman Catholic Church in the United States spoke directly to the morality of same gender orientation. The Bishops' Committee on Marriage and Family of the National Conference of Catholic Bishops issued a statement titled "Always Our Children." This was a very carefully considered and worded statement which came out of five years of consultation with experts, pastoral ministers, parents, and the Bishops' own Committee on Doctrine and Pastoral Practices. In it the Catholic Bishops explain clearly their understanding about the moral issue, and I quote: "Generally, homosexual orientation is experienced as a *given, not as something freely chosen.* By itself, therefore, a homosexual orientation cannot be considered sinful, for morality presumes the freedom to choose."[6] (Italics added.)

The Catholic Bishops issued their statement to the parents of children who are gay, hoping to relieve parental anxiety concerning the morality of same gender orientation. One does not need to be a Catholic to take comfort from their clear, unambiguous conclusion: Gender orientation is *not* a choice.

If you have read my brief autobiographical sketch in the introduction, you already know that life taught me that same truth long before I ever knew Dr. Money's name or the Catholic Bishops issued their statement. For nearly four decades I struggled to become the well-adjusted heterosexual male which society said I should be. Clearly, I preferred to be straight. I chose to be straight so many times over so many years that even God has lost count.

And what was the net result of all that effort? In the final analysis, nothing changed! I remained the gay man I had always been. Gradually, I came to accept reality—the reality that I had no choice, that what I preferred simply didn't matter. Finally, I accepted the fact that my need to love and be loved was grounded in an orientation toward persons of my own gender.

5

What Determines Orientation?

How I wish I could answer that question. I can't, but neither can anyone else with any sense of intellectual honesty. The fact is, modern science does not yet know precisely how orientation is determined.

Countless pages have been written in the past century setting forth the proposition that environmental factors determine orientation. Such theories are collectively referred to as "social determinism." Generally speaking, they hold that life experiences during childhood and adolescence set the stage for one's orientation.

Standing in opposition to those theories is the school of "biological determinism." Generally, it holds that orientation is determined prenatally (i.e., before birth) by a combination of genetic and hormonal factors. According to biological determinism, we all come into this world with a predisposition toward either heterosexual, homosexual, or bisexual orientation.

From two such diametrically opposed positions, it isn't hard to understand what fuels the "nature versus nurture" debate in America today. Personally, I believe Dr. John Money is correct in saying that "the only scholarly position is to allow that prenatal and postnatal determinants are not mutually exclusive."[7] By that statement, he means that biological and environmental factors *both* play a role in the orientation one comes to have. Specifically, he holds that nature and nurture interact during some critical developmental periods, and that the resulting orientation tends to persist immutably thereafter.[8]

I suspect that in the future we'll have a more definitive answer as to what actually determines individual orientation. For now though, we're stuck with ambiguous statements like the one I wrote for a position paper in 1991: "Orientation arises out of a complex interplay between genetic, hormonal and environmental factors—a phenomenon not yet fully understood." Unfortunately, that's still all I know to say today.[9]

6

Is Same Gender Orientation a Mental Disorder?

Historically, same gender orientation was considered a mental disorder by both the American Psychiatric and the American Psychological Associations. Gay individuals like myself were described in such unflattering terms as "abnormal," "deviant," "perverse," "pathological," and even "schizophrenic" (which basically means to be out of contact with reality). Needless to say, such an assessment by the doctors of mental health dealt a devastating blow to our self-esteem.

Speaking for myself, I emerged from adolescence in 1960 with such concepts firmly fixed at all levels of consciousness. The books I was able to find on college shelves during the decade that followed only reinforced those same assumptions—that I was a sick, degenerate individual in desperate need of cure.

Imagine, if you will, the excitement and relief I experienced in 1973 when the American Psychiatric Association reversed itself, voting to remove homosexual orientation from its list of psychiatric disorders! And less than two years later the American Psychological Association did likewise. Overnight, it seemed to me, the mental health community had come to its own senses, conceding that persons of same gender orientation were not ill simply because of their orientation.

Finally, others were saying what I already intuitively knew about myself—that my interest in other men was not a matter of mental illness at all, but merely an aspect of my own unique personality. With that knowledge came the beginnings of liberation and hope, and eventually, the ego-strength to discover myself fully and to live authentically.

So where does the issue stand today, a quarter century after those ground-breaking decisions? Thankfully, the position taken in the early 1970's remains unchanged, and those who know the most about mental health no longer consider same gender orientation to be a mental disorder.

7

Is Same Gender Orientation a Spiritual Disorder?

Stated differently, can an individual be gay, live openly as a gay man, and still be acceptable to God? I have decided to include this controversial question because it plagues so many individuals dealing with the issue of orientation, gay and straight alike. For those of us who are religious, how God really feels about gay orientation is an extremely important question. The answer, of course, is highly individualistic and seems to depend primarily upon one's religious upbringing and personal experience of God. That means any answer one gives is inevitably grounded in his or her own life story.

One would think a person with my background would find it easy to tell his story, that is, to speak of his experience of God. Yet I have found this question extremely difficult to discuss. I have delayed and postponed sharing the details of my spiritual journey as long as possible, still fearing what others will think and say when they see my words in print. Nevertheless, for me to speak openly of my walk with God is the only possible way you can understand the ground upon which my spirituality rests.

In the pages which follow I shall make every effort to respect your theological tradition and not to argue for one point of view as opposed to another. Instead, I will use the space to share what I personally know of God, and trust you to draw whatever conclusions you feel appropriate.

§ § §

The earliest memories of my Methodist heritage date back to my kindergarten years in the deep South, and by the age of six or seven I was ringing the church bell every Sunday morning. I loved to ring that bell and waited patiently by its rope for the head usher's nod. I also loved my church. It was a comfortable place to be. The people were warm and caring, and God was viewed as a compassionate, loving Father[10] who accepted all persons unconditionally. At least, that's how nostalgia chooses to have me remember it.

But of one thing I am certain: my Southern Methodist tradition was quite ambiguous concerning same gender orientation during my formative years, preferring to leave the subject simply unmentioned rather than condemn anyone. Never once during my childhood or adolescence do I recall a Methodist minister making prejudicial statements about persons of gay orientation. Never once. In retrospect, I realize I was spared a lot of grief by Methodism's tolerant attitude.

Such was not the case with society at large, however. With the exception of my church, there seemed to be universal condemnation toward homosexuality. I was dismayed, not really knowing whom or what to believe. At least, that's how it felt as I suffered through adolescence and into the early years of college. Then came the crisis over Michael. I simply must tell you that story, for it led me to my first real life-changing encounter with God.

We must go back thirty-five years to a cold winter night in 1963 when I isolated myself on a dormitory rooftop. I had to escape for a while. I couldn't allow any human being to know my real feelings for Michael. He also was a college junior and my best friend, but I wanted so much more. I wanted to spend all my time with him, to tell him my innermost secrets, to hold him and have him hold me. I was obsessed with Michael and thought of little else. He was more than merely a friend, and certainly far more than the object of my sexual fantasy. I was falling in love with Michael!

I had gone to the rooftop that night feeling condemned. No, not by God, but by the composite social forces which had brutalized my spirit. In spite of the gentle ways of my Methodist heritage, I doubted who I was, my value, and my acceptability to God. It brings me to tears just remembering the confusion, shame and guilt I felt that night. In 1963, young men simply did not allow themselves to love other young men. My anguish was overwhelming. I simply had to get control of myself before something terrible happened.

"Going to the rooftop" was really nothing new for me. Since childhood I had been finding quiet places to be alone with God in times of trouble: the deserted streets of our town on which I took long walks late at night; the sanctuary of our church, to which I had a key; even my own bed with the covers pulled over my head. God was present in all those places, offering comfort and peace. But never was the divine presence more pronounced than on the rooftop that clear, cold, moonless night in February of my junior year.

My body shook and my cheeks were wet with tears as I prayed for forgiveness and strength. I don't know how long I knelt there crying, but I shall never forget the moment when divine assurance rose up from the depth of my soul. In a way that defies human explanation, I felt God saying, *Terry, listen to me. Stop crying and listen to me! I love you just as you are—whatever your orientation proves to be.*

Well, needless to say, God had my attention! As I continued to listen, I felt God's spirit saying *Terry, start loving yourself. Treat yourself and others with dignity and respect. And trust that I will be with you always ... no matter what.*

For over three decades now I have cherished what happened there that night, for it gradually changed my life. As I read back what I have written here, it brings tears to my eyes time and again. I feel chills just remembering the night I first experienced God as a truly imminent deity who resided not transcendently on some other side of the universe, but at the core of my very soul. And the God of my soul was no passive bystander who looked on disinterestedly as I experienced the pain of that night. Rather, God experienced that pain with me and assured me that life held potentials which I had not yet prehended.[11]

At the time I had none of the words nor philosophy to explain what happened on that rooftop, but I came away from the experience knowing I had been embraced by divine love and that the Lord God of all creation wanted me to love myself as well.

But therein proved to be the problem. Love myself? Yes, I wanted to, but that could only happen when I became straight, when I became the well-adjusted heterosexual male which society expected me to be. Sadly, I missed God's call to authenticity that night. Apparently I missed it for many years to come, because I left that rooftop engaged in a struggle against God which was to last a full quarter century.

Only recently have I begun to realize the depth of my rebellion, of my unwillingness to heed God's call to authenticity and self-acceptance. As I now see it, I fought God every step of the way. Becoming straight was such an obsession, such a driving force, that it obscured the very truth God most wanted me to understand about myself.

Instead of allowing God to help me write a script for my own unique life, I felt compelled to live out the script prepared by my heterosexual culture. I learned to deny my most basic feelings—including my feelings for Michael and the other potential Michaels who followed. I worked my way on through college, seminary, and eventually into the ordained ministry of the church. Marriage came soon thereafter, and in the years that followed, the birth of three wonderful children.

I remember so much joy when I reflect back across those years. Yet I must admit that the joy was tempered by a constant crisis within my soul. Rather than heed God's call to honesty and self-exploration, I engaged in one addictive detour after another in an attempt to escape how I really felt. I wasted enormous time and energy simply refusing to actualize the authenticity to which God called me. Frankly, I seemed determined to escape myself at any cost.

Then came the day in 1972 when my own United Methodist Church voted to clear up its ambiguity concerning same gender orientation. The governing body decided it "could not condone homosexuality," declaring it "incompatible with Christian teachings," and prohibiting the ordination of gay clergy.[12]

I felt betrayed and saddened beyond words when the church I loved—the church which had historically championed human rights—voted to take a discriminatory position against persons like myself. As I saw it, their position was based on such a distorted view of scripture and tradition that it failed to distinguish between mature, same gender orientation and the irresponsible, violent sexual behaviors purportedly characteristic of the men in Sodom and Gomorrah (see Genesis 19). Although no one knew my true orientation at the time, I was judged and found unacceptable by the well-intentioned but ill-informed men and women of United Methodism.

I am still unclear how deeply that action affected me. Yet through it all God remained faithful, assuring me that my acceptability to him did not depend upon the church, nor upon what the church thought. God was always as near with guidance and strength as my willingness to ask. Indeed, God was near even when I had little or no conscious prehension of divine presence. I now realize that in the midst of what felt like absolute chaos, there was a divine order urging me onward toward the future, toward authenticity with its gift of spiritual, emotional, and physical well-being.

Yes, standing above and beyond the madness of daily living was the divine call to authenticity and self-love. It seemed as if God never missed an opportunity to remind me of what he most expected— that I was to be *Terry*. Ultimately, he would accept nothing less.

Well, what more can I tell you that isn't already self-evident? Obviously my power was not sufficient to sustain the struggle against God's creative spirit. Against my will, God led me into full recognition and gradual acceptance of my gay orientation, then out of a life-long closet into full disclosure, and eventually into the authorship of this book. With the Psalmist of old, I affirm this day that "God is my portion; he has been my savior."

Accordingly, no dictate of society, no doctrine of the church, no opinion of any individual will ever persuade me that same gender orientation is a spiritual disorder. God himself has convinced me otherwise. In the midst of a hostile environment, God has constantly been there, assuring me of my innate worth and of his love for my gay soul.

So, what do *you* think? Is same gender orientation a spiritual disorder? The answer is one you must find for yourself, and I offer my story as a stepping stone on your journey toward that end.

8

Can Orientation Be Changed?

There are two prominent schools of thought in America today which contend that orientation can be changed: specifically, reparative and conversion therapies. We need to look at each briefly and with as much fairness as possible.

The term "reparative therapy" is currently popular among some mental health professionals. It holds to psychoanalytic theory from the 1950s and 1960s—namely that male same gender orientation is a developmental disorder which generally results from inadequate bonding between father and son. Based on such a premise, the practitioners of reparative therapy have devised treatment programs aimed at helping what they call the "non-gay homosexual" behave heterosexually.

To the best of my knowledge, the chief proponent for that school of thought is Joseph Nicolosi, a Ph.D. psychologist who practices in California. In a 1991 publication titled *Reparative Therapy of Male Homosexuality*, Dr. Nicolosi explains his position and sets forth both the goals of therapy and his methods of treatment.[13] He is currently executive director of NARTH—the National Association of Research and Therapy of Homosexuality. The association reports a membership of 500 nationally and is dedicated to helping the homosexual change.

Obviously, there are a sizeable number of mental health practitioners who believe that same gender orientation is a mental disorder for which treatment should be available. They believe the mental health profession has basically abandoned the homosexual who seeks help, and are determined to provide therapeutic services aimed at helping such individuals become heterosexual.

Standing in clear opposition to such thought, however, is the full weight and prestige of the 150,000-member American Psychological Association. As recently as August 1997, its Council of Representatives overwhelmingly passed a resolution reaffirming the association's longstanding position that homosexuality is not a mental disorder. Moreover, the resolution stated that the APA "opposes all portrayals of lesbian, gay and bisexual people as mentally ill and in need of treatment due to their sexual orientation."[14] It raised ethical concerns about any attempt on the part of psychologists to change their clients' orientation, and specifically named "reparative therapy" as suspect.

The resolution went on to suggest that attempts to change orientation are motivated by "societal ignorance and prejudice," and called on mental health professionals to "take the lead in removing the stigma of mental illness that has long been associated with homosexual orientation."

And as if all that were not enough, the mental health community is only one battleground where the war rages as to whether or not orientation can or should be changed. A similar conflict is taking place between Christian fundamentalism and the more liberal theological community. I'm speaking, of course, of the conflict over what has become known in recent years as "conversion therapy."

A substantial movement has arisen within ultra-conservative churches the past decade to offer a healing ministry aimed at curing individuals of homosexuality. Those ministries are based on the presupposition that healing can occur because same gender orientation is a spiritual disorder. That is, they hold that gender orientation is a choice, and to choose to participate in homosexual behavior is a sin which God will overcome through divine grace once the gay person sincerely repents.

The idea that homosexuality is a sin which can be healed by God is a persuasive argument to an individual suffering from the negative pressures of our heterosexual society, and those who advocate such a philosophy do so with great skill. Because they claim to have the strength and power of God in their ministry, they appeal to the vulnerable, hurting individual, whether it be the gay man himself, or a family member or friend who loves him and wants to see him healed.

The largest and best known ministry which purports to "heal" gays is Exodus International, and persons who have been through its conversion therapy program typically refer to themselves as "ex-gays." It has chapters around the country and operates on-going support groups to help individuals avoid "relapsing" into homosexual behavior.

The question, of course, is whether or not conversion therapy actually changes orientation, or simply modifies behavior for a period of time. According to Gregory M. Herek, Ph.D., the claims of "successful conversions" by religious conservatives are anecdotal in nature and filled with methodological ambiguities. He states:

> In many published reports of "successful" conversion therapies, the participants' initial sexual orientation was not adequately assessed. Many bisexuals have been mislabeled as homosexuals with the consequence that the "successes" reported for the conversions actually have occurred among bisexuals who were highly motivated to adopt a hetero-sexual behavior pattern.
>
> An additional problem is that "success" usually has been defined as suppression of homoerotic response or merely display of physiological ability to engage in heterosexual intercourse. Neither outcome should be equated with the adoption of a complex set of attractions and desires that con-stitute sexual orientation.
>
> Many interventions aimed at changing sexual orientation have succeeded only in reducing or eliminating homosexual behavior rather than creating or increasing heterosexual at-tractions. They have, in effect, deprived individuals of their capacity for sexual response to others.[15]

I'm sure it will come as no surprise to know that I agree with Dr. Herek. What's going on here is really pretty simple: relying on behavior modification as its primary tool, "conversion therapy" uses the powerful forces of guilt, and the promise of freedom from guilt, to entice the gay individual into a complex web of self-denial and outright repression of his true orientation. As we shall see in chapters eleven and twelve, the orientationally repressed gay male is typically capable of entering heterosexual marriage and performing sexually *as if* heterosexual. Such behavior is inherently dishonest, however, and it proves to be at great cost to everyone's well-being as the repressive syndrome begins to give way to reality.

Because I believe God wants gay individuals to reach orientational authenticity, I contend that the internal questions arising from orientational confusion are God's Spirit working to lead the person toward that goal. To take advantage of this spiritual seeking through false claims of a divine "cure" is to work counter to the work of God in the individual's life. At the moment when the individual is most open to God's Spirit, these programs attempt to reinstate the very repression God is attempting to lift.

I believe treatment programs based on the concept of "conversion therapy" are dangerous to the spiritual and mental health of the very individuals they attempt to "cure." Furthermore, I believe the American Psychological Association took the position it did in the summer of 1997 in an effort to discourage any and all such attempts, regardless of the philosophy used to justify them. Conservative Christians who offer ministry to heal gays, however well intentioned, are trying to do what the mental health community clearly rejects. I submit that attempting to sell a gay man the false hope that he can "stop being gay" is basic dishonesty, and that to victimize such individuals at their point of greatest vulnerability is spiritual and emotional abuse!

Although I'm certain the views expressed above will prove unpopular in many circles, I do not

personally believe gender orientation can be changed—
either by "reparative" therapy, "conversion" therapy,
medication, or individual will power. I have drawn this
conclusion after spending the first half of my own life
trying to change my orientation, and watching
countless others attempt to do likewise. Subjectively
speaking, none of us appears to have lastingly altered
our orientation. On an objective level, I have seen no
evidence based on creditable research of lasting,
authentic change.

Whatever the cause or causes of orientation may
actually be, it appears to be fixed for life even before
we develop a conscious concept of sexuality. I'm saying
that we grow up gay, straight, or in-between, and
nothing changes that fact, ever. We do ourselves and
others a great injustice by denying reality and holding
to the illusion that orientation can be changed.

9

Does Orientation Determine Sexual Behavior?

Most of you reading this book are straight and have had little reason to ever distinguish between orientation, (which is our need to love and be loved by a gender-appropriate partner in a committed, on-going relationship) and sexual behavior (which is the type of sexual activity in which we actually engage at a particular moment in time). Being straight, you've always known your deepest need for love has been toward persons of the opposite gender, and pursuit of that need has received social approval and life-long reinforcement. In conformity with social expectations, you have sought to marry, raise children, and find a way to "live happily ever after." You have lived and loved in ways consistent with your deepest emotional needs. Your orientation has directed your sexual expression, and as a result, you have known the joy of congruence.

Many of us, however, have lived a life characterized by incongruence. That is, we have desired one thing, yet felt compelled to do another. The distinction between innate orientation and sexual behavior is so crucial that Dr. Money illustrates the point by the so-called "skyscraper test." I quote:

> A sexual status (or orientation) is not the same as a sexual act.... The Skyscraper Test exemplifies the difference between sexual act and sexual status. One of the versions of this test applies to a tourist with a homosexual status who is atop the Empire State Building . . . and is pushed to the edge of the parapet by a gun-toting crazed sex terrorist with a heterosexual status. Suppose the homosexual is a man and the terrorist a woman who demands that he perform oral sex with her or go over the edge. To save his life, he might do it. If so, he would have performed a heterosexual act, but he would not have changed to have a heterosexual status.[16]

The point is, some of us are forced by life into sexual behavior which is inconsistent with our true orientation, with our basic feelings and desires. The coercive force may be either physical or emotional, or both. It may force us into an isolated act or a persistent pattern of behavior. In any event, we are behaving sexually in ways incongruent with our basic orientation in order to survive, in order to meet the expectations of those individuals and/or social forces which control the moment.

As we shall see in the chapters which follow, such is the case for gay men who marry women. The coercive force is a homophobic society which victimizes everyone in its path by insistence upon strict compliance with its heterosexual norm.

10

What Is Homophobia?

Homophobia is the fear society has instilled in most of us toward persons of same gender orientation. Based on the false premise that orientation is a choice, homophobia is grounded in the culturally reinforced belief that homosexual individuals are inherently defective and somehow dangerous to society at large.

For the first seventy-five years of the twentieth century, such thought went almost unchallenged in America. Homophobia was essentially institutionalized, with the laws of government, the doctrines of religion, the theories of mental health, and even the movies of Hollywood, all portraying gay individuals as emotionally ill and morally irresponsible. Strict penalties were prescribed for persons either unable or unwilling to conform to the heterosexual norm. To be outed in America meant loss of respect, often the loss of job and family, and occasionally the loss of life itself. There were few, if any, positive gay role models to be emulated and few places in social thought for the concept of mature, responsible same gender orientation.

Only in recent years have I come to understand that my parents were victims of such social prejudice, and more importantly, the extent to which I internalized their homophobia. You recall from chapter one the story of my neighborhood friend's father who was purportedly arrested for "something sexual involving another man." Well, little did my parents know that in condemning him, they were condemning their own six-year-old son as he eavesdropped on their late-night kitchen conversation. They had no idea that I heard the anger and hatred in their voices as they pronounced judgment on a man they hardly knew. Assuming their eldest son to be straight, they could not have known the terror their words and attitude struck at the core of my very being.

I suspect many of the details associated with that whole experience remain deeply repressed within my psyche, perhaps never to be fully recovered. But this much I do know: I came away from that kitchen doorway deeply ashamed of myself and filled with guilt. I somehow knew that I had feelings of the sort which had brought condemnation upon my friend's father, and I simply could not allow his fate to become my own.

I believe it is accurate to say that homophobia drove me so deeply into my own closet that I scarcely cracked the door for almost three decades. The social costs of being gay were just too high, the penalties too severe. From that night on, I was determined to hide my true feelings until I found a way to change—until I found a way not to notice other boys. I lived in constant fear of discovery, knowing full well that disclosure of my thoughts and desires would bring certain condemnation and perhaps outright abandonment.

Moreover, I felt there was no one to talk to, no one in whom it was safe to confide. I believe homophobia deprived me of the normal ebb and flow of emotional security which should have characterized childhood and adolescence. It forced me into an isolation where God alone became my only trusted confidant.

By the time I reached adulthood, homophobia was thoroughly internalized at all levels of my psyche. That is to say, I had come to feel about myself the way I perceived society felt about persons of same gender orientation—*I had come to hate myself, and deeply feared my own God-given orientation.*

It is hard to overstate the devastating impact of such self-hatred upon the development of the gay psyche. As a practicing psychotherapist, I have come to believe that internalized homophobia engenders severe shame and self-hatred in virtually all gay men. Unfortunately, the condition is seldom recognized either by the individual or by society, and even less often is its cancerous effect really understood.

11

How Does Internalized Homophobia Affect Gay Men?

This is a relatively simple question with a *very* complex answer. You see, not all gay men respond to the self-hatred of internalized homophobia in the same way. As society becomes increasingly tolerant of same gender orientation, it appears that an increasingly large number of young gay males are confronting homophobia head on. They somehow refuse to allow the powerful forces of social conditioning to dictate their attitude about themselves. Not only do they learn to accept their gay orientation without apology, many find ways to live honest, open, authentic lives.

Such is not yet the case for most of us, however. In the pages which follow we shall look at three self-destructive responses far more typical of gay males in American society: 1) youth who commit suicide long before reaching adulthood; 2) chemically addicted young adults who die from drug or alcohol abuse; and 3) gay married men like myself who assassinate emotional authenticity for the sake of physical survival.

Gay Youth and Suicide

I know this is a painful place to begin, but we desperately need to confront the fact that gay youths appear three times more likely to commit suicide than their straight counterparts.[17] That means, according to a federal government study, some two thousand young gay men and lesbians are taking their lives annually. Imagine a large high school with a student body of two thousand with all its students suddenly disappearing, or a large auditorium seating two thousand with all its seats empty. What we have here is a national tragedy. Year after year, two thousand young people simply vanish unnecessarily from the face of the earth while most of us manage to look the other way.

According to the Missouri Department of Social Services, we here in the Kansas City metropolitan area have one teen suicide every eight days![18] Your community has its own statistics, and if recent findings of the University of Minnesota are correct, gay males in their teens are seven times more likely to attempt suicide than their straight counterparts.[19]

In 1997 this hard reality was brought home to me in a very personal way. Several young gay men helped me review the manuscript that was to become this book. As they read and responded to the text, I heard the same comment time and again—most had seriously considered suicide at some point during their teen years. Some had attempted it. Growing up gay in America, it seems, is often just too hard to face.

It saddens me to think I might never have known these fine young men, or never have heard their stories. But they are the lucky ones, the survivors. There are many other stories which will never be told—never told because we stood by passively while the evil of overt homophobia led the would-be story teller to a premature grave.

Young Adults and Chemical Addiction

Then too, there are countless thousands drawn into a more subtle form of suicide—namely, chemical addiction. These young men typically are well aware of their gay orientation and attempt to escape the self-hatred and shame of internalized homophobia through drugs and alcohol. Some drink themselves to death in quiet isolation, never telling anyone the deep secret they attempt to drown with alcohol. Others tend to make the gay bar the center of life, turning the unique social opportunity it offers into an excuse for participation in an epidemic of drug and alcohol abuse estimated to be three times the national average.[20] I suspect that figure may actually be low.

Denied self-contempt drives such individuals to live on the edge, and to link their sexuality to drugs and alcohol in such a way that they become increasingly impotent unless high. Sadly, they tend to go from one sexual partner to another, and from one short-term pseudo-relationship to another, in a desperate search for love and acceptance. They become increasingly empty and seldom find satisfaction beyond the moment. Not believing they deserve the relationship for which they long, they sabotage themselves at every point, often falling victim to unprotected promiscuous sex and its lethal consequence—AIDS.

As I see it, such young men are driven by what Freud called "the death instinct,"[21] driven to destroy themselves one way or another. Hope gradually gives way to severe depression as drugs and alcohol increasingly fail to relieve their pain.

For reasons hard to identify, it appears that the majority of young gay males use and/or abuse drugs and alcohol for years without becoming chemically dependent, eventually putting those behaviors behind them. Still others "bottom out" at some point. They enter a twelve-step recovery program and begin the long climb to sanity. Far too many eventually die, however, either from a drug overdose or the effects of chronic alcoholism.

I realize what a negative picture I'm painting of chemically addicted gay males who make the bar the center of life; but frankly, I'm probably not stating the case strongly enough. As a therapist, I know first-hand of the broken lives and chronic unhappiness that lie beneath the plastic smiles and GQ appearance of such young men. Sadly, very few seem willing or able to confront the internalized homophobia which drives their desperate attempts at self-escape.

The bottom line is this: Without treatment and sustained recovery, alcohol and drug addiction are one hundred percent fatal.[22] The disease is progressive, and the day comes when its victims simply aren't there any longer.

Married Men and Orientational Repression

We now turn to a radically different response which many individuals take when faced with the self-hatred of internalized homophobia. Specifically, I'm speaking of gay men like myself who enter heterosexual marriages and father children, believing this is the only way we can become productive members of society. How, you ask, can all that possibly happen?

In a word, we manage to commit a different type of suicide. Believing ourselves to be flawed, defective people with inappropriate feelings, we gradually manage to kill emotional authenticity rather than the body. We assassinate our true selves (that is, what psychology calls the ego) and seek to become the persons that our families and society say we *should* be (that is, the person envisioned as "ideal" by the superego).

To be quite specific, the process of ego annihilation begins when we knowingly and intentionally force unwanted thoughts and feelings from conscious awareness into what is commonly called semi-consciousness. Once suppressed, our needs and desires for intimate relatedness to persons of the same gender aren't there to be contended with on a daily basis. Temporarily, we "forget" what we "know," forcing it into the shadows of awareness. When the pain and confusion of those unwanted emotions attempt to resurface into consciousness, we simply push them down again. That's suppressive denial. As Scarlet O'Hara said at the end of *Gone with the Wind*, "I'll think about that tomorrow."

All of us use suppression throughout life to cut reality down to a manageable size. That's normal, and we probably could not maintain good mental health without it. The problem is, suppression alone gradually proves inadequate to protect the gay psyche from the extreme anguish associated with internalized homophobia. What we "want to forget" keeps erupting into awareness, insisting that we listen to ourselves. Such self-awareness proves too much for many of us. The pain becomes too great. We need a defense mechanism far more powerful than mere suppression to obliterate the shame and self-hatred which lie at the core of our being.

Relief finally comes when suppression begins to give way to repressive denial. It is as if a trap door opens un-noticed, dropping painful, unwanted emotions to a depth of the psyche far beyond the reach of conscious awareness. Our most painful thoughts and feelings are involuntarily locked away in the archives of our unconscious selves, often never to be directly encountered again. Moreover, we even tend to lose awareness that a conflict ever existed. Through a process beyond our control, what we once knowingly and intentionally held in semi-consciousness simply disappears—at least for a while.

In his book *Uncharted Lives*,[23] Stanley Siegel describes just such a process within himself. As adolescence gave way to adulthood, he knew less and less of his authentic self with regard to orientational status. Gradually, conscious awareness of his desire to love and be loved by another man disappeared. He entered a heterosexual marriage, became a father, and gained prominence as a mental health professional specializing in marriage and family therapy. I believe Stanley Siegel, like most gay men who enter heterosexual marriage, was in repressive denial of his true orientation.

All of this leads me to the following hypotheses: *Once suppression gives way to a sufficient level of orientational repression, most gay men are capable of entering* *heterosexual marriage and appearing totally straight.** In regard to gender orientation at least, it is as if the true self (that is, our ego) is rendered inert by the culturally imposed beliefs and behaviors by which we feel compelled to live. What the true self feels and wants no longer matters. In fact, it is no longer consciously known. At this point, the assassination of authenticity is complete and a false self emerges. For all intents and purposes, the gay man appears straight, even to himself.

---

*For a more detailed discussion of Orientational Repression and its effects on gay men, see Appendixes A and B.

12

Why Do Gay Men Enter Heterosexual Marriages?

Gay men who enter heterosexual marriage in their teens or twenties do so overwhelmingly as an act of social compliance. They are typically in massive denial of their true orientation, having worked for a decade or more to banish from conscious awareness all knowledge of their need to love and be loved by another man. In the process, they have tended to become what others want them to be at the sacrifice of their own authenticity.

I want to be perfectly clear: I am saying that virtually all gay men who marry at the socially appointed time believe themselves to be straight, or at least "straight enough" to make heterosexual marriage work. They want their share of the great American dream—a wife, children, social and professional acceptance, financial security, and above all, love. Moreover, they are driven by the same basic instinct for bonding which motivates all of us to form primary relationships.

When orientationally repressed gay men marry, they do so with the full expectation of making the marriage work. I'm saying there is no charade, no conscious knowledge of an intent to deceive. They take the vow "until death do us part," truly believing that only death can separate them from the women they love. Even those who have been aware of an on-going sexual attraction to other men typically sign that interest off to "bisexuality," believing all such attraction will cease to exist once they are happily married to the right woman.

For a personal account of the powerful forces compelling gay men into heterosexual marriages, I recommend *Stranger at the Gate* by the Reverend Mel White. Particularly insightful are chapters two through five in which Rev. White candidly shares his journey from the early years of adolescence through the early years of marriage. It's all there in clearly written autobiographical style—the struggle, the pain, the desire to do God's will as he then understood it, the determination to be straight, and the belief that what he really needed to "get over this homosexual thing" was a to marry "a good woman."[24]

I know many of you will view all this with doubt and suspicion, not quite believing that persons like Mel White and me could be that cut off from our true selves. Unfortunately, the account is all too true, not only for us, but also for the vast majority of gay married men whose stories I have heard behind the closed doors of the counseling suite. Only much later, as orientational repression begins to lift, do we discover how badly we have unknowingly deceived both ourselves and others. (If you have not already done so, I encourage you to read the preceding chapter on "Homophobia." You will see how it sets gay men up for the pseudo-heterosexualism of orientationally repressed adulthood.)

Finally, a personal note before we move on. Merely to say I'm angry at the way we've all been victimized by the rigid heterosexualism of Judeo-Christian America is a gross understatement—I am enraged! Nothing about the assassination of a gay man's authentic orientation is fair, and nothing about its life-long impact on the family he loves is fair. Unfortunately, the damage is done long before the individual has enough ego-strength to face the truth about himself, much less to live congruently. I only hope this book will help lift us out of the ignorance which continues to perpetuate the marriage of gay men to unsuspecting women.

13

Why Do Gay Men Allow Themselves to Become Fathers?

The vast majority of gay men are in denial of their true orientation when children begin to be born to the marital unions into which they have entered. Believing themselves to be straight, they embrace fatherhood in the same way their heterosexual counterparts do—with a mixture of absolute joy and fear of parental inadequacy.

To some extent, I believe, the birth of children actually solidifies the gay man's heterosexual myth about himself. He finds he loves his children dearly, is willing to sacrifice virtually anything for their well-being, and takes all that as proof positive that he is straight. "After all," he asks, "would a gay man have such devotion to children?"

The answer is *Yes*! Most of the mature gay men I have known want children, and when blessed with them, experience the same love and devotion as mature straight fathers. From the emotional point of view, I am convinced there is little if any difference between gay and straight fathers with regard to their desire for children or their ability to parent.

Once I assumed that the intense love I felt for my own children was probably somewhat unique among gay men, that I would not likely find others who shared my experience of fatherhood. I could not have been more wrong. I have counseled extensively with dozens of gay fathers across the years, and I know first-hand the way most feel about their children. I see them share the joy of their children's achievements and the pain of their children's failures. I often hear gay men tell me how thankful they are to be fathers, but never once have I personally heard a gay father express regret over bringing children into the world. Never once.

Admittedly, the self-referred gay clients with whom I work professionally may not be representative of society at large. They are, nevertheless, the sample from which I've drawn my conclusions, and I find virtually all tend to be outstanding fathers. By and large they are sensitive, caring individuals who are highly invested in their children's lives. And, as we shall see later, most actually come to view voluntary disclosure of their own gay orientation as "an act of love" toward the children they have fathered.

Finally, a word about gay men who would like to be fathers. Through the years I have also had the opportunity to counsel extensively with a large number of unmarried gay males, men who somehow manage to avoid the orientational repression which led their heterosexually married counterparts down the church aisle. For many the probability of remaining forever childless is the one regret they express concerning their gay orientation. "I just wish I had children" is a phrase I've heard time and time again in counseling sessions with unmarried gay men.

All this leads me to conclude that while those of us who are gay may be less than enthusiastic about the type of sexual behavior required to bring children into the world, we covet fatherhood nonetheless. And when blessed with children, most of us do all we can to become good parents.

14

When Do Gay Men Typically Discover Their True Orientation?

I believe virtually all gay men have an innate sense of their same gender orientation in childhood. They find themselves drawn far more to boys than to girls, and in a way they intrinsically know is "different" from the natural curiosity of their peers. Realizing their feelings and desires are socially unacceptable, they are driven to hide those feelings, even from themselves.

The process of denial is insidious, and full repression of their desire *to love and be loved by another man* occurs across decades, rather than resulting from a single traumatic event. Ever so gradually, they know less and less of themselves as congruence increasingly defers to the pressure for social compliance. Ever so gradually, all that remains in conscious awareness is a limited knowledge of *sexual interest* in persons of their own gender. Convincing themselves that such sexual interest has nothing to do with love, they successfully suppress even those emotions most of the time, believing that all attraction to other men will cease to exist once they are happily married.

With perhaps rare exception in the more liberal closing decades of the 20th Century, virtually all gay men who dutifully marry in their late teens or twenties are victims of orientational repression. They are cut off from themselves emotionally as a result of the suppressive and repressive denial that has characterized their lives for so many years. So successful is that denial that most have lost the very knowledge of themselves that initially instigated the process itself. Accordingly, they show up at the church on time, faithfully take their wedding vows, and fully expect to live a heterosexual life-style thereafter.

Sadly, many do just that. They remain repressed for the balance of their natural lives, never finding the ego-strength to face the truth about themselves. Psychology generally refers to such persons as "latent homosexuals," those who believe themselves to be straight when the opposite is actually the case.

I have no idea what percentage of orientationally repressed gay men eventually rediscover the truth about themselves. However, I am convinced that the recovery of one's lost gay self is *a developmental task of mature adulthood*. When such discovery does occur, the process typically gets underway in the individual's mid to late thirties and goes on for a full decade or more. The journey inward requires enormous ego-strength and rigorous self-honesty. You see, coming to know and accept one's repressed gay orientation is inevitably a difficult, confusing, and prolonged task.

As perhaps you will recall from chapter one, I first identified myself as bisexual to my former wife in 1975. I was 33 years of age. Such self-identification proved to be an important step in the process which eventually led to full acceptance of my gay orientation. But that acceptance did not come for another ten long years.

From my professional work with other gay men, I have gradually learned that the process we all go through is remarkably similar, and the timing is almost identical. Typically, discovery begins to occur only after a decade or more of successful marriage and numerous career achievements. It appears that those very relationship and workplace successes may be crucial in helping the orientationally repressed gay male develop the ego-strength eventually to face the truth about himself. Whatever the factors which facilitate the lifting of repression may be, of this much we may be certain—only the most hearty souls complete the journey inward and return to disclose voluntarily their true orientation to the people they love.

So, you ask, when do gay married men discover their true orientation, their long-denied need to love and be loved by another man? Some never make the discovery, but rather enter their graves in the same repressed state that characterized their entry into marriage. Others do make the discovery, but the process is inevitably long and painful, not only for the gay man himself, but also for the family he has helped create.

15

What Happens After Discovery Occurs?

Some married men who come to discover their gay orientation apparently exercise enormous self-control, never acting to meet their most basic emotional need—the need for a primary relationship with a life-mate gender-appropriate to their true orientation. Moreover, some have reported to me that they fully intend to remain sexually faithful to their wives at all costs, never acting to meet even the sexual component of their life-long desire.

However, my work with an increasingly large number of gay married men over the past decade has led me to conclude that such is seldom the case. My clinical experience has led, in fact, to the following hypothesis: *Once gay married men recognize their true orientation, there appear to be four developmental stages through which mentally healthy individuals progress as orientational authenticity evolves. They are: (1) the sexual exploration stage; (2) the intimate relationship stage; (3) the community affiliation stage; and (4) the spiritual integration stage.* Let us now look briefly at each of these stages.

The Sexual Exploration Stage

During the *Sexual Exploration Stage*, the vast majority of gay married men are absolutely determined to remain with their families indefinitely, persuading themselves that sexual gratification alone is sufficient expression of their newly discovered gay orientation. Most find ways to fulfill occasionally their desire for sexual contact with other males, but without revealing either their true identities or admitting (usually even to themselves) the extent to which their behavior is driven by the need to love and be loved by a gender-appropriate partner. Constantly vacillating between the suppression of reality and orientational authenticity, they convince themselves time and again that such behavior is "sex for sex's sake," and that they will never allow it to interfere with the heterosexual marriages to which they remain committed.

To state the obvious, the sexual exploration stage is a time of great turmoil, of betrayal, of enormous guilt, and a time when the risk of disease from anonymous sex is extremely high. Men who participate in such behavior constantly fear that they will contract HIV infection, that their promiscuous ways will be discovered, and that they will eventually hurt and lose the very individuals they love most—their families. Yet they continually find themselves driven to act out sexually with other men, regardless of the potential cost.

During this stage, families invariably sense that something is wrong, but have no idea what. Typically, gay married men are emotionally absent from the family interactions in which they superficially participate, and loved ones begin to suspect that they are either depressed or suffering from a presumably unidentified mid-life crisis. As wives begin to pick up on their husbands' increased emotional and physical unavailability, they tend to blame themselves for their husbands' behaviors, and often wonder if their husbands are having extramarital affairs with other women.

To reiterate, the sexual exploration stage is a chaotic time when issues remain unclear and the wrong questions are asked. Unfortunately, the chaos often goes on for years, and no one is quite sure what creates the family dysfunction in which everyone participates—save the gay married man himself.

The Intimate Relationship Stage

The *Intimate Relationship Stage* begins when gay married men come to realize that neither they nor their families can go on this way indefinitely, that something has to change. By this point most are keenly aware that random, anonymous sex is ultimately empty and unfulfilling. The first real change comes when they begin to turn away from those old patterns and increasingly seek sexual expression within the context of an emotionally intimate relationship. In fact, the establishment of such a relationship typically becomes the primary goal of the men who manage to reach this stage. They desperately want to be known, accepted, and hopefully loved for the individuals they actually are, not the persons they have always pretended to be. If any single need characterizes stage two, it is the need for genuine emotional intimacy with a gender-appropriate partner. Typically, such intimacy actually becomes *more* important than sex itself to the maturing gay male.

As the quest for authenticity intensifies, it gradually pervades virtually all aspects of the gay married man's life. Most men find themselves increasingly determined to live honest, open lives wherever possible. It is at this point that many gay married men voluntarily come out to a few trusted friends beyond the immediate family, often to their wives, and occasionally even to their own children. With or without a primary same-gender relationship, they seem determined to move from deception to integrity by finally allowing the people they love most to know the truth.

The road map through the intimate relationship stage varies considerably. After voluntarily disclosing their gay orientation, some men move rather quickly to establish a residence separate from their families and make themselves available for the love relationships they have always needed. Others disclose their true orientation to the families they love, but remain in the home until such time as they meet the individual whom they believe to be the long-sought life-mate, the individual with whom they wish to live and build a future. In some cases, the intimate relationship they desire never occurs and the marriage remains intact, ending only with the death of either spouse. And far more often than one might expect, there are even those gay married men who bond in an on-going same-gender relationship while remaining with their family—often with the full knowledge and consent of their heterosexual wives.

The point is, once the truth is on the table and wives finally know what they are really dealing with, different couples work out different transitional patterns. The transitions are never easy, of course, but at least now the chaos has a name and energy can be used toward addressing the real problem rather than the smoke screens which have characterized the past.

For those couples who wish to remain together and better understand the wife's perspective on the coming-out process, I recommend two books in particular: *When Husbands Come Out of the Closet* by Jean Schaar Gochros, Ph.D.[25] and *The Other Side of the Closet* by Amity Pierce Buxton, Ph.D.[26] Chapter two of Dr. Buxton's book should be especially helpful in that it specifically addresses "alternative marital styles" designed "to accommodate gayness."

The Community Affiliation Stage

The *Community Affiliation Stage* comes as quite a surprise to most gay married men. It appears to evolve whether or not they have managed to establish a gender-appropriate intimate relationship. The stage begins when the gay individual takes steps to affiliate openly with some aspect of the gay community— something the vast majority of gay married men thought they would never do. This stage is a time when gay married men essentially come out within the gay community. Such disclosure arises from the need for non-sexual, platonic friendships with other gay men like themselves. They desperately want to be known and accepted for the persons they actually are, and that can happen only in a group setting where they are free to be fully honest, fully disclosed.

In most cases the establishment of an on-going gender-appropriate relationship during stage two delays somewhat the on-set of the community affiliation stage. In time, however, most gay couples make the transition into the gay community, becoming increasingly open concerning their orientation and their relationship to each other.

But the real surprise comes when these men discover the desire for greater disclosure yet. Being out to their immediate family and the gay community proves inadequate as the community affiliation stage continues to evolve. They find themselves driven toward full public disclosure of their gay orientation. They find themselves no longer willing to hide— period. They are gay, and they are ready for members of their extended families, for friends and work associates, for *everyone* to know the truth.

Not all gay married men evolve to such a high point of orientational authenticity, but those who do certainly find their families greatly alarmed. You see, it's one thing to disclose voluntarily to one's family, and even perhaps to the gay community; but it's quite another thing to make a full public disclosure. With good reason, families typically find the community affiliation stage very threatening.

The Spiritual Integration Stage

The *Spiritual Integration Stage* is without doubt the least recognized, but ultimately the most important stage of all. In this stage gay men come to experience their orientation as a God-given, sacred blessing. Gripped by divine love, gay men experience the shame and guilt of internalized homophobia gradually giving way to genuine self-acceptance. Joy replaces depression and life takes on new meaning. It becomes increasingly important to treat both themselves and others with dignity and respect. All things seem to be dramatically transformed as love becomes a way of life, and most striking of all is the transformation from self-contempt to authentic self-love. It is at this point, I believe, when orientational authenticity can be called "mature" or "fully evolved."*

§ § §

In conclusion, I want to emphasize that not every gay married man who comes to recognize his true orientation moves through these four stages in a sequential, linear fashion. Many individuals become stuck along the way, only fantasizing as to what they wish could be. Moreover, regression is not uncommon, when progress toward authenticity gives way to fear and guilt, causing hard fought gains to be lost as the individual slips back into the deceptive behavior of the past.

"Torn-ness" marks every step of the journey, and the path traveled is so individualistic as to make any generalization or construct only partially helpful. Each man evolves in his own way, at his own pace, and only to the level of his own potential.

---

*For a more detailed discussion of the Spiritual Integration Stage, see Appendix C.

16

Why Do Some Married Men Fake Straight After Discovery of Their Gay Orientation?

While writing this book, I must have asked myself a thousand times why I continued to fake straight so long after discovering my gay orientation. The answer is remarkably simple: I loved my wife and children and I feared what would happen to them if the truth were known. I believed coming out would destroy their world, that it would create pain and suffering from which they might never recover. Faking straight seemed like the kindest thing to do in those days, the only responsible course of action.

But I must also admit that I feared for my own well-being. I believed I could not live without my family—without Mary, David, Annika and Tom. I was dependent on their love, and felt convinced that disclosure of my true orientation would make me an outcast, that I would lose them ... forever.

Faced with that much fear, it isn't hard to understand why I sought to hide the truth from the people I loved the most. I didn't want to hurt anyone, including myself! As a result, I knowingly and intentionally entered the closet all the more deeply once my orientational repression began to lift. I was determined to maintain the pseudo-heterosexualism which had always characterized my life. I was convinced beyond doubt that such behavior was a courageous act of love, that I was protecting my family from the devastation I believed disclosing the truth would bring.

To suggest that men like myself intentionally fake straight to protect the families we love will undoubtedly be a difficult concept for many of you to accept. As I have counseled increasingly with gay married men across the years, however, I have come to realize how truly representative my own story actually is. Time after time I have heard one man after another echo sentiments which once sprang from my own heart. Certainly, their words were characteristic of my own past, and I knew exactly what they meant by statements like "Dr. Norman, I think I've finally accepted the fact that I'm gay, but I still love my wife and children. I would rather die than hurt them!"

More could be said about all this, but saying more would only tend to complicate the issue. The fact is, gay married men who intentionally fake straight for a period of time after discovering their true orientation do so to protect both themselves and the families they love. It's simply part of the process through which we move as orientational authenticity evolves, and for my own years of deceptive behavior, I personally make no apology. Strange as it may sound, I actually look back upon that time with a sense of satisfaction and pride.

To this day, I believe I did the right thing by withholding the truth until my family and I had the strength and maturity to face it.

17

How Could I Have Been
So Naive?

I suspect there's a strong chance you're feeling rather naive, wondering why you didn't realize for so long that the gay man in your life was faking straight. Now that you know the truth, you're likely feeling angry and victimized. The result of such deception can be devastating. It destroys our ability to trust others and even to trust ourselves.

At least, I know that's how my brother felt at the time of my disclosure to him in the fall of 1990. Shortly before his untimely death seven years later, I shared with him the first part of this book. In response, he sent me an open letter which conveyed some of his own thoughts and feelings. He gave me permission to use this material anyway I saw fit. I'm ready to share some of what he wrote with you now. I will let Jim's own words speak for themselves:

"To say I was surprised when Terry told me he was gay would be the understatement of the century. I had been brothering with this man for 41 years, and thought I knew him as well as any person could know another; yet I can think of nothing that would have surprised me more than the morning he told me he was gay and planned to 'come out' in the near future. ... In retrospect, I realize my first thoughts were very selfish. Would our friends think that I was gay also? Would my 14-year-old daughter be exiled by her friends? What would my wife think? Could I ever trust this person I thought I knew again? He was even in my will as the custodian of my child!"

Obviously, Jim had no idea that I was gay. Even though we were close as brothers and spent time together almost daily as children, adolescents and adults, he had no clue about my same gender orientation.

How could he have been so naive? The answer is simple. Gay men like myself have learned to become invisible by successfully blending into the heterosexual culture around us. Our very survival demands it. The Kinsey Institute estimates that only one in seven of us exhibits any of the stereotypical traits normally associated with same gender orientation.[27]

Moreover, most of us disappear not only from those who love us, but from ourselves as well. As you already know from the earlier discussion on the effects of internalized homophobia, most gay married men live for years in a state of orientational repression. During that time we become very skillful at playing the role of a heterosexual man. After repression begins to lift, most of us continue playing this role as long as possible to protect ourselves and those we love.

If you, like my brother, were surprised when a family member disclosed his same gender orientation, you're not alone. If you feel angry and hurt by this deception, you're not alone. If you are asking yourself how you could not have known about the gay man in your life, you're not alone.

But I strongly suspect you *feel* alone. The number of families faced by this dilemma is one of the best-kept secrets in America. Dr. Tex Sample, who wrote the preface to this book, considers the secrecy maintained by gay married men and their families one of the few remaining closets in American society. Dr. Sample is both a theologian and a nationally known sociologist. For three years he served as a member of the study committee on homosexuality of the United Methodist Church. As I prepared the text of this book, he expressed the belief that at any point in time no fewer than twenty million Americans are affected by some aspect of this phenomenon.

Twenty million Americans is a staggering figure. Dr. Sample understands, of course, that such a number is merely an estimate. In fact, all statistics about same gender orientation in general and gay married men in particular are estimates. No one knows for sure how many Americans are same gender oriented or how many married men are gay. Part of the problem with any study concerning same gender orientation is the difficulty in defining the population. Some studies consider a person gay if he or she has occasionally engaged in homosexual behavior. Other studies count only those who identify themselves as gay.

As you can imagine, many people are very reluctant to discuss either their behavior or their gender orientation with anyone conducting a survey, thus frustrating the researcher's efforts at accuracy.

Therefore, conclusions can vary widely based on the questions asked and the willingness and ability of survey participants to answer honestly. These uncertain results can confuse and bewilder anyone searching for concrete answers. For example, the estimates of individuals with homosexual orientation in America range from 10 percent in the famous Kinsey reports to less than 3 percent in a report by the National Research Center at the University of Chicago.[28]

Given such statistical confusion, it really isn't possible to give an exact figure as to the number of families who face a dilemma like your own. Scientifically reliable data simply does not yet exist. I can tell you only that number is staggering.

It's easy to understand, of course, why we all tend to want such statistics. Knowing we aren't alone helps a lot. Knowing that others have faced and survived orientational transition can provide significant comfort.

In the end, though, the real question you need to ask is not how many gay married men there are in America, but how many there are in your household. If a married man in your family has come out to you, the answer is: *one*. This one man and the family he loves are more important than any statistic, and no generalization can take away the pain brought on by the disclosure of his same gender orientation.

The one sure fact is that you now know the truth, since the gay man you love is no longer faking straight. Let's turn now to the process that brought about voluntary disclosure and try to understand how such a thing came to be.

18

What Is Voluntary Disclosure, and What Motivates the Disclosure Process?

By "disclosure" I mean the process by which the outside world comes to know the gay married man's true orientation. There are two basic types of disclosure: involuntary, in which the individual is outed by circumstances beyond his control; and voluntary, in which the individual intentionally reveals his gay orientation as an act of conscious choice.

It is easy enough to understand the forces behind involuntary disclosure. It can occur in any number of ways. For example, a gay married man's true orientation could become public knowledge when he's arrested for some illegal sexual behavior. Perhaps the health department calls with notification that he has contracted a sexually transmitted disease from a gay partner. He could be discovered in a compromising situation by a neighbor who feels compelled to inform his wife. Maybe a jealous lover calls or writes the gay married man's wife, informing her of her husband's secret life. When confronted with such involuntary outing, the gay married man is forced from the closet by circumstances beyond his control. He has no other choice.

But what can possibly explain *voluntary* disclosure? What motivates gay married men to come out of the closet when external circumstances don't appear to demand such action? What leads them to upset the status quo of home and family, to be willing to thrust everyone and everything into chaos in order to pursue what is commonly called a "gay life-style"? To the heterosexual observer, such behavior must appear absolutely insane.

I wish I could tell you that my own voluntary disclosure in 1990 was a matter of great personal maturity and outstanding ego strength; but in all reality, it was a matter of sheer survival. I believe God used the Grim Reaper to drive me from the closet just before work and food and alcohol addictions took my life. But you need to know how I arrived at those conclusions. Once again that means sharing a painful part of my life journey in considerable detail, then allowing you to draw from it those parallels which apply to the situation you face.

§ § §

The journey began in the early 1980s as I began doctoral work at Saint Paul School of Theology in Kansas City. Before we proceed, however, you need to see "Terry" as I saw him at the beginning of that journey. I was thirty-nine years old, weighed an ideal one hundred fifty-five pounds, wore thirty-two-inch trousers, tapered shirts and European-cut Pierre Cardin suits. The eating disorder and low self-esteem which had plagued my family of origin seemed to have passed me by. I recall my banker once describing me as "looking like a Philadelphia lawyer." My physical appearance and emotional demeanor spoke of success; in fact, I had succeeded at virtually everything I had undertaken. I had been successful in the ministry, in real estate development, in the graduate study of counseling psychology, and I certainly saw myself as an outstanding father.

I had often been accused of having more than my share of arrogance and egotism, and in retrospect, that was probably an understatement. As I moved on to become "Dr. Norman," it was with full confidence that I could control myself and face any situation the future might bring.

As my doctoral studies formally began, one of the first books I purchased from the seminary bookstore was a groundbreaking paperback by Dr. Don Clark titled *Loving Someone Gay*[29]. It was the first book I had encountered that presented gay orientation in a positive light. I was shocked to find it, and even more shocked to read what felt like my own story unfolding in its pages.

Here was a gay man who had lost his sense of orientational identity, married and become a father, only to rediscover himself for the gay individual he had always been. He then managed to disclose his true orientation and went on to become the author of the book I was reading! As I devoured *Loving Someone Gay*, I realized I needed to do just that—and the someone I needed to love ... was me.

I think Don Clark's book had a lot to do with the lifting of my own orientational repression. I became determined to love myself for the gay man I was, and to accept my need to love and be loved by a gender-appropriate partner. But I was equally determined to remain in the closet, never allowing for the gratification of that need. To protect my family, I would fake straight indefinitely, regardless of the potential consequences to my own health and well-being.

The decision to "know myself," while living a life incongruent with that self knowledge set me up for a decade of internal conflict which almost took my life. I began a love-hate relationship with myself. I felt like a union of opposites, torn constantly by the ambivalence between accepting and rejecting my very being. The more I named and claimed my true self, the more I discovered the shame and self-hatred of internalized homophobia which lay embedded at my very core.

Rather than thrive, I began to self-destruct. As the months turned into years, I worked more and more, never exercised, ate three times the number of calories necessary to sustain life, and drank on a daily basis. Needless to say, my body suffered terribly. The beginning of the end came on December 28, 1988. In retrospect, I realize that's the date when my ability to fake straight really began to crumble.

Yes, I remember the exact day perfectly. Mary and I were at the hardware story picking up things for a weekend "do-it-yourself" project when my pager went off. Jim, my younger brother by five years, had just been admitted to the local hospital and was in the midst of a major heart attack.

I recall being out of breath as I rushed my own two hundred-fifteen-pound body to the intensive care unit. I also remember wondering how this could possibly be happening to my forty-year-old brother. He had always been in such good health, and it was almost incomprehensible to find ourselves in a hospital waiting room a few days later while he underwent quadruple bypass surgery.

I remember that long wait, and I recall thinking to myself how easily I could have been the one undergoing that surgery. Like I said, I was five years older, many pounds heavier, and far less physically fit than Jim. As the hours slipped by, I decided to make a New Year's resolution—I would cut back on the hours I worked, find time to exercise regularly, begin eating properly, and lose fifty pounds in the year ahead. I felt determined to take much better care of myself, determined to do all within my power to insure that Jim's fate did not become my own.

What I remember most following Jim's heart attack, however, was the intense pressure I felt from others to have a complete physical myself. I finally agreed, and what a shock it was a few weeks later when I developed arrhythmia while undergoing a routine tread mill test there in my doctor's office. As if that weren't enough, my heart rate reached a dangerously high level and simply refused to slow down. "Terry," Dr. Bregant said, "I want you to go to the hospital. We really need to check this out."

Sanity would have suggested following medical advise, right? But no, not me! I had too much to do, too many people who depended on me, and far too much pride to admit that I was sick. I clearly recall saying, "No hospital, Bob. Let's deal with this on an outpatient basis."

Fortunately, my heart slowed to a normal rate within the hour, and Bob did allow me to leave his office. But I left with two medications that day— Propranolol, for high blood pressure, and Lanoxin, to control arrhythmia. All this hit me really hard since I had always been unusually healthy. It was my first bout with significant illness and the first medication I'd been directed to take on a sustained basis, ever.

"Obese." That was the diagnosis Dr. Bregant used to describe my physical condition that day. Me, obese? I could hardly think the thought, much less face the fact that my five-foot, eight-inch frame carried a full two hundred-fifteen pounds. What was I doing to myself, and why?

I don't believe I ever told anyone what really took place during that physical. I felt too ashamed. I didn't want to admit that portions of my life were out of control, that I had literally made myself sick. But the fact is, I had done just that. I look back on the work load I carried during the years preceding that physical in utter amazement. I was a husband and the father of three, a son to my own aging parents and son-in-law to Mary's folks (all of whom lived in the community), the director of a counseling center where I saw twenty or more clients a week, the pastor of a 250-member congregation which underwent a major building restoration during my years there, and all while I was working my way through a doctoral program in pastoral psychology. No wonder I was sick. No sane human being should take such a load upon himself.

Motivated by the fear of death, I left Bob's office determined to take control of my life, determined to see things change. But the only thing that changed was my waistline. It continued to grow as I continued to eat. I could hardly believe the scales as I eased up a pound or so with each passing month. I don't recall cutting back on work either, and I'm absolutely certain there was no sustained effort at meaningful exercise.

I shall never forget the stern warning from my wife's mother as I filled my plate for a third time at a Holiday Inn breakfast bar one morning. "Terry," she said, "You are digging your grave with your teeth!" As angry as those unsolicited words made me, I knew she was right.

As if that weren't enough, there was . . . the beer. For years I had been bringing home a six-pack several nights a week, and gorging down several cans in my basement study while my unsuspecting family slept upstairs. Though it's hard to admit, beer had become my beverage of choice, and many of the extra pounds I carried to that tread mill test were the direct result of my secret, late-night drinking.

And when I didn't have the privacy of my study in which to drink, I would occasionally drink in the privacy of my car while "running errands." I felt terrible about what I was doing, of course, and constantly feared what would happen if "the Reverend Dr. Norman" was arrested for driving while intoxicated.

One such occasion of drinking and driving stands out above all others. My oldest son, David, was perhaps 12 or 13 at the time, and we had spent several hours shopping for the perfect pair of basketball shoes.

I don't know how many beers I had behind David's back that afternoon, but gradually I became intoxicated, and my patience ran its course. While lecturing at the top of my lungs about his "impossible to please attitude," I reached across the car seat and slapped David in the face! I can still see his little body as he pulled away from me, hunkering against the passenger door in a fetal position. There was no way David could have known he was the recipient of his father's lifelong rage that afternoon, and that his Dad's behavior actually had little if anything to do with him.

With regret and humiliation, I have apologized to David more than once for what took place on that shopping trip. Interestingly, he has no memory of the event. Just as Barbra Steisand sang in "The Way We Were," it really seems that "what's too painful to remember, we simply choose to forget."

But I haven't forgotten. I haven't forgotten physically abusing my own son, driving while intoxicated, or drinking myself to sleep night after night. At the time I knew I had become psychologically addicted to alcohol, using it habitually to escape feelings I didn't want to feel. The question was, had I become physiologically addicted as well? Was there really a genetic predisposition toward alcoholism which caused the body to become chemically dependent on the substance in order to function? Did I have such a predisposition? Was I an alcoholic?

I denied that such was the case, however, persuading myself time and time again that I would eventually stop drinking, that I was only using alcohol temporarily to relieve the pain I felt deep inside. But I drank like an alcoholic, and I knew full-well that any competent clinician assessing my drinking patterns would make a diagnosis of alcoholism. What was the truth? I had no way of knowing, since I either would not or could not stop drinking for more than three or four days at a time.

I remember the shame and self-loathing I felt as I looked at my fat, aging face in the bathroom mirror every morning. While shaving, I promised myself day after day that I would really get serious about dieting and exercise, and that I would stop drinking too. I would do it "tomorrow." Tomorrow, of course, never came. In spite of my brother's heart attack, my own declining health, and my mother-in-law's stern warning, I continued to eat and drink as if there were no tomorrow.

My level of fear and preoccupation with death increased as I found myself less and less able to control my food and alcohol intake. With each additional pound, I seemed more isolated from others. The excessive weight must have made me less attractive to my wife, and I know it served as a "shield of blubber" to keep any would-be gay lover at arm's length. I became increasingly non-sexual to the outside world, depending on gay pornography and the fantasies of my mind for sexual gratification, knowing full well that none of those fantasies would ever become reality. The truth is, I lived alone in the prison of my own fat body and warped mind, believing that life had passed me by, and wondering if I would live to see another birthday.

Against all odds, I somehow did make it through another year. On my forty-seventh birthday, I tipped the scales at two hundred-thirty pounds, had begun buying clothes at the Big and Tall Shop, and found forty-two-inch waist trousers uncomfortably tight. I felt terrible about myself. Although I was desperate to take control of my life, I had no idea how.

For years my pain had produced some of the best sermons and finest counseling I had ever done. I remember thinking of myself as the doctor who could heal others, but who could not heal himself. I felt powerless to free myself from the downward spiral in which I was caught. I experienced the whole situation as absolutely hopeless, and saw no reason for optimism as my forty-eighth year of life began.

The tension between accepting myself for the gay man I was and maintaining a pseudo-heterosexualism for the benefit of my family had proven too much. The love-hate relationship I felt toward myself had taken a heavy toll, and I knew something had to change—one way or another. I simply could not go on this way. Period.

Finally, change began to happen, but in the most unlikely of ways. A copy of the big book for *Overeaters Anonymous* mysteriously turned up one day on my desk. I still have no idea who left it there, but as I read its pages, I began to understand that I had become addicted to food. Food had become my escape, the primary means by which I attempted to alter reality. I was using food in an effort to fill the emotional emptiness I felt deep inside. I obsessed over what I was going to eat next, and when I overate, I obsessed over my guilt at having done so.

The fact is, I had become an addict. Food had become the "drug of choice" which I used habitually to escape the feelings associated with my orientational dilemma. I had developed a pathological relationship with food, the lethal side effects of which were gradually destroying my life.

And as the pounds accumulated around my waistline, shame and self-contempt continued to accumulate deep within my soul. As I focused on food and what overeating had done to my physical well-being, I escaped temporarily the real feelings which had driven those very eating behaviors—the fact that I hated myself for being gay, and deeply resented my inability to develop a healthy, enduring self-love.

Once I understood my addictive relationship to food, it was only a small step to apply that new knowledge to alcohol. Alcohol's ability to alter the reality I sought to escape was immediate and powerful. It lifted my inhibitions and replaced my pain with a sense of artificial well-being which often lasted for hours. No wonder I had become psychologically dependent on alcohol. It was a great fix—except that it really fixed nothing and brought with it life-threatening problems of its own.

Ah, and finally, I understood why I had been such an adherent to the Protestant work ethic. Forever, work had been my saving grace. If I stayed busy enough, there was little time or energy to experience my own true feelings. Yes, I came to see myself for the workaholic I had always been, and when work alone ceased to provide adequate escape from the feelings I didn't want to feel, I cross-addicted. I began to use food and alcohol to augment my workaholism. Together the three almost did me in!

Looking back on all this, I have come to believe that once my orientational repression began to lift, I went through a decade-long grief process. With the knowledge and acceptance of my gay orientation came great loss. Gone was the heterosexual script around which I had always organized my life. It no longer applied to me, and I had no idea what my script as a gay married man should be. Gone too were the missed opportunities for authentic relationships which repression had denied me. Those years could never be reclaimed. I felt angry and cheated, and felt that in my ignorance I had unintentionally victimized others as well. And, as if all that were not enough, there was the anticipatory grief of future loss, should my gay orientation eventually become a matter of public knowledge.

All this led to bouts of depression which were almost too much for my weakened ego. Endlessly, it seemed, the stages of grief fed back upon themselves as I cycled from denial to anger to depression, all the while constantly bargaining with both myself and God, trying to find an acceptable way out.

I hesitate to speak of God again, but honesty requires me to do so. You see, during all those years of emotional trauma, God was always there, always whispering words of divine wisdom from the very core of my soul. I knew God loved me, and I knew he wanted me to understand, accept, and love myself. Moreover, I felt God wanted me to be honest with others, to have the courage to tell the truth. In the midst of trouble valley, I was never far from the divine hand. And *always* it seemed to be leading me toward authenticity.

But I was such a rebel. I simply could not accept the fact that God accepted me, just as I was, gay and all. While I attempted to comply with God's will in other areas of my life, I fought him every step of the way in regard to my orientation. For over a quarter of a century I had preached that truth had the power to set us free. Yet I resisted allowing it to heal my own broken spirit.

In retrospect, I believe I bottomed out in the early spring following my forty-seventh birthday. I realized that the secret I was keeping had made me physically and emotionally sick. I came to believe that the death instinct of which Freud spoke described me perfectly, that I was in the final stages of self-destruction.

I believe it's accurate to say that I turned my life over to God as never before during the early spring of 1990. I accepted the fact that I was powerless to change my orientation, and powerless over the addictions which had developed to obscure it. I accepted the fact that my daughter would have to have an openly gay father walk her down the aisle, or by the time she was ready for marriage, she would have no father at all.

I'm sure it's obvious to you by now that the "voluntary" disclosure which followed during the summer and fall of 1990 wasn't so voluntary after all. God really did use the Grim Reaper to drive me from the closet just before work, food, and alcohol addiction took my life. Apparently, God was determined to have me live, and in the final analysis, that meant that I had to be *Terry*. Thankfully, God would accept nothing less than my full authenticity—and with it, I was to learn, came the precious gifts of spiritual, emotional, and physical well-being.

So, you ask, what motivates voluntary disclosure? For me, it was the will to live, the desire to stay alive. I'm saying *survival* is the motivating force behind intentional disclosure, and survival ultimately necessitated telling the truth.

Although the details vary from one gay married man to another, I am convinced that a prolonged grief process virtually always follows the lifting of orientational repression, and that the constellation of addictive escapes are virtually always there, mutating endlessly in their effort to keep us from authenticity. Given all this, it's a wonder of God that any of us survive to tell the truth, much less to write stories like the one you have just read.

19

What Possible Good Can Come from Voluntary Disclosure?

Voluntary disclosure of my gay orientation to my family and friends was undoubtedly the most difficult thing I've ever done. The pain we all suffered during the fall of 1990 was so great I often wondered if anything good could result from such a process. My wife clung to my words of fifteen years earlier, remembering how I had said "I think I'm bisexual, but I'll never allow my interest in men to interfere with the well-being of our family." Fifteen years later there I was, telling her how wrong and naive I had been, that I was "gay through and through," and that I couldn't go on with my heterosexual charade any longer.

Disclosure threw our lives into greater and greater chaos as the process gradually evolved. The status quo was turned upside down, and the denial of emotion quickly gave way to unbelievable anger as we found ourselves gripped by fear. A racing mind, forgetfulness, the inability to concentrate, a predisposition toward accidents, loss of appetite, sleeplessness, waking up in a cold sweat from relentless nightmares, intense anxiety, outright panic—my wife and I experienced them all as we attempted to comprehend what disclosure would mean to our family's future.

In spite of what I believed to be divine assurance that I was doing the right thing by coming out, I found the process almost more than I could handle. Constantly, I doubted if anything worthwhile could possibly arise from the devastating pain we all felt. I kept asking myself if all this was really necessary, if there wasn't a less painful way. For a decade I had been protecting my family by intentional deception; now, it seemed, I was destroying them with honesty. As the process of disclosure moved forward, I felt increasingly unsure of myself, ready to crumble at any moment. What's more, I knew it was worse yet on my wife.

I mean, it was one thing to confide the truth to Mary and a few trusted friends. (I actually think we handled that relatively private stage of disclosure pretty well.) It proved to be quite another thing, however, when I began to move from *limited disclosure* to what eventually became *full public disclosure*. That's the point at which life began to spin out of control, the point at which I wanted to stop the coming out process dead in its tracks, to re-enter the closet and pretend as if I were the straight man others had always assumed me to be.

"Terry, you simply have to go on telling the truth. A couple of years from now everyone involved will be better off." Those were the words of encouragement from our friends Robert and Sharron Cook in the fall of 1990 as I wanted to back away from disclosure, as I desperately wanted to recant the words I had already spoken. "But Mary deserves to know the truth," they insisted, "and you deserve an opportunity to live your own life. Just tell the truth, and in time the pain will pass."

As I had anticipated, coming out to Robert and Sharron had been easy enough. They were insightful, accepting, and supportive. The Cooks had been family friends for over twenty years and loved us all unconditionally. They knew our family as they knew their own, both its strengths and its weaknesses. We had camped and vacationed together, celebrated birthdays together, and I even had baptized their oldest son. Now we were hurting together, as they empathetically shared our pain. Yet through it all they remained remarkably focused, insisting that I "just tell the truth," insisting that full honesty was our best hope for the future.

As you already know, I believe God struggled for years to lift me from the orientational repression into which I had fallen, and then struggled to save me from the life-threatening addictions which replaced repression. It seemed that God was always there, urging me to know and accept myself and to live a responsible life congruent with that self-knowledge. Now here were Robert and Sharron encouraging me to do the same. At the point when the pain of disclosure was greatest, the point at which I most wanted to back away, it seemed that God brought living, breathing individuals into my life to reiterate the holy word, to encourage me to trust the truth arising from my own soul.

Clinging to the hope that Robert and Sharron were right, clinging to the hope that my prehension of divine will was accurate, I eventually came out to my brother, to my professional colleagues at the counseling center, to my physician and my attorney, and to an increasingly large number of personal friends.

To my astonishment, what developed for us was a community of support, as one person after another took a position similar to that of Robert and Sharron! Rather than being banished for my gay orientation, I found myself loved and accepted by virtually everyone who had loved and accepted me prior to disclosure! The truth is, none of the terrible things I had always imagined came to pass. Our family and friends proved remarkably understanding and stood by us every step of the way. I began to realize how truly kind and caring others were proving to be, and that coming out was the beginning of a new era, not the end of the world.

Energized by the acceptance and support of persons who I had historically believed would reject me, I eventually found the courage to face my worst fear of all—coming out to my own children. Mary and I had agreed that Tom, just seven at the time, should be told only that we were separating, and not why. But we agreed that both David and Annika should have the whole truth, and that they should hear it from me.

I know what I feared most was the impact disclosure would have on their lives. David was within one semester of high school graduation, and Annika was a sophomore. They were doing well both academically and socially, and I feared coming out would destroy their world, that disclosure was the right thing, but at the wrong time. Yet everything in my own life seemed to have brought me to this very point, and I couldn't turn back now. Telling David and Annika the full truth was my only real option.

To grasp the dynamics of the situation, you need to understand that my children and I had always been extremely close. We spent a lot of time together and spoke openly about the issues they faced on a daily basis. I'd often felt that the emotional intimacy that characterized our parent-child relationship was truly outstanding, that we loved each other unconditionally, and that nothing could ever destroy that bond. Now it was time to put all that to the test. Did I really trust their unconditional love for me? Did I really trust that nothing would separate us permanently, including the disclosure of my gay orientation? Did I trust them enough ... to tell the truth?

I know I have set you up to expect a detailed account of that disclosure event itself. The fact is, however, I have not yet been able to recall the exact details of what I said, or even when and where I said it. I recall only that the conversations took place, and that the initial shock was so severe that both David and Annika refused to see me for several days thereafter. The pain we experienced was so traumatic that all three of us have totally suppressed the detail—a coping mechanism with which you should be thoroughly familiar since you have read this far. Yes, Barbra Streisand was correct in our case: The things that were too painful to remember, we simply chose to forget.

For me, David and Annika's initial reaction was undoubtedly the darkest moment of the entire disclosure process; but thankfully, the dark cloud soon proved to have a silver lining. Within a week's time the isolation we first experienced began to give way to the deepest, most authentic conversations I had ever had with either of them. Not only did the love David and Annika had for me survive, but they began to ask questions which revealed a genuine desire to understand their father. And as the weeks passed, their newly acquired understanding brought with it the beginnings of outright support. They seemed to grasp the fact that voluntary disclosure was somehow an act of love, and that eventually, we'd all be better off.

I know the process was terrible for them, of course—much worse than either David or Annika let me know at the time. Only later did I learn the extent to which they held back many of their feelings in order to spare their mother and me additional pain. From the onset, their primary concern seemed to be for our well-being, and they supported us both unconditionally, somehow managing never to take sides.

No, I didn't lose David or Annika as a result of disclosing my gay orientation, nor did my coming out bring their world to an end. They recovered from the shock of their father's unexpected news with remarkable grace, and went on with their individual lives. The whole experience proved to be much different from what I had anticipated. The storm came, but it also passed, and with its passing came a new era—one characterized by total honesty and unconditional positive regard, the benefits of which we had only begun to realize.

Surprisingly, what happened with David and Annika repeated itself time and again as the disclosure process continued to evolve. I believe it is accurate to say that virtually all the relationships I valued most gradually improved as I openly shared the deep dark secret of my gay orientation with family and friends.

Sometime during the fall of 1990, I began to realize just how correct Dr. Carl Rogers had been in suggesting that congruence on the part of one individual tends to facilitate congruence in others.[30] That is to say, the more honest we are with ourselves and others, the more likely they are to be honest with us in return.

I doubt that anything could have driven that point home more dramatically than my own brother's response to disclosure. Within a week following verbalization of my historically unspeakable secret to Jim, he told me his own seemingly unspeakable secret. No, Jim wasn't gay. His secret had nothing to do with sex. It concerned a humiliating event from his late teens which he had always assumed he would never tell anyone—and now here he was, telling his gay brother!

Jim and I continued to be together often until his untimely death in 1997, but never again was there anything we could not say to one another. I know the relational authenticity we came to value so much took root on the very day I spoke the words "Jim, I'm gay." Coming out to Jim brought with it a level of emotional intimacy I would never have dreamed possible. Finally, we were brothers not by blood only, but by a bonding of souls which resulted from absolute honesty.

Often my brother and I speculated about how our parents would have responded, had they been alive at the time of my disclosure. "You know Mom and Dad would have accepted your orientation just like I have. They wouldn't have understood, or necessarily approved, but they would have gone on loving you ... gay or not." Yes, those were the words I heard from Jim on several occasions. Given the fact that so many others seemed to go on loving me unconditionally—gay or not—maybe, just maybe, Jim was right.

At any rate, there was no doubt about Jim's love. Once he began to understand my situation, he became a strong advocate of outright public disclosure. He shared my story with his own wife and daughter, and eventually, with his own friends. I was amazed that Jim showed no shame or humiliation over having a gay brother, and that he actually supported me and my family as the coming out process proceeded.

Even Jim's wife, Debbie, proved to be an advocate of authenticity in ways I would have never expected. Raised as a conservative Baptist in the Deep South, she invited me into their home "for as long as you need to stay" when the time of separation from Mary finally came. As you will learn later, I accepted that offer and stayed in their home many nights over the next two or three years. For a short while, I even considered it my primary residence for legal purposes.

All the while my wife's family and friends were supporting her in a similar way. That was particularly true of her younger sister, Barbara, with whom we both had many long and tearful conversations. It seems to me it was with Barbara the way Jim said it would have been with my parents. Although she didn't completely understand or approve of what was taking place, she nevertheless managed to love and support both her sister and me unconditionally. Not once do I recall feeling judged or condemned by her. Without taking sides, she did everything within her power to help us through what felt like an impossible situation.

But I'm sure you want to know more about how the marital relationship evolved as my coming out process became more and more public. As I remember it, our very worst times came with the approach of the holidays in the final weeks of 1990. For so many years, my wife and I had lived under the illusion that we could and would go on together indefinitely. But gradually the conspiracy of silence concerning my orientation began to evaporate. Gradually I was changing all the rules, insisting that we face the truth, and demanding the freedom to explore my gay orientation fully. As unfair as it all may have been, I increasingly gave my wife no choice other than to adapt to the transition through which I felt determined to take us. I felt she gave me no choice other than to go on with the charade I believed our marriage had become.

I'm sure there is no way Mary and I will ever fully understand how each other felt. Often we tried to talk, but our efforts at honest communication usually deteriorated into shouting matches which lasted until I walked out of the room. I know I was scared to death at what the future would bring to me, my wife, and our children, but that fear often camouflaged itself as hostility and anger toward her.

I believe Mary did all within her power to keep the marriage from ending. I look back on the pain I put her through in our final weeks of living together with deep, deep regret. It seems as if the battle lines had been drawn, however, and we could do little more than fight. If I had known then what I know now, perhaps I could have been fully honest without throwing us into that level of emotional chaos.

What I know for sure is that I did not conduct myself during those final weeks as I would have liked. I spoke the truth all right, but with what now seems like unnecessary brutality, then simply walked away in an effort to preserve my own frail ego.

I don't want to give the impression that Mary never said or did anything during those weeks that hurt me. She often said and did things that hurt a lot. But she also continually found ways to express her heart-felt concern for my well-being. She spoke of love very seldom in our final days together, yet to my utter amazement, I *felt* loved and cherished by her even during our darkest moments, even when the heat of our arguments was the most intense.

And I still loved Mary. I recall with clarity my desire to assure her that my love continued, but I had come to understand the real nature of that love. I loved her as the person with whom I had shared emotional and physical intimacy for over twenty years. I loved her as the mother of our children. I loved her in many ways, but it was not the love of a husband for a wife.

Sadly, I failed miserably to convey most of this to the woman who was still legally my wife, but with whom I could no longer live. I don't believe she felt at all loved by me. I believe she felt deceived and betrayed and tended to blame herself for not being able to stop the inevitable.

But the inevitable came for us after the children left for school the morning of December 3, 1990. With no strength left to fight, I loaded my bags into the car and drove to my brother's home some ten minutes away. The drive seemed to last forever, and I knew full well that it was taking me down a path from which there was no return.

What would the new era really be like for all of us, and was it true that lasting good would arise from the ashes I had created? Only the future could answer that question.

The days following separation required many decisions. It was time to face the counseling center board of directors, the administrative board of Russellville Church where I'd served as pastor for almost ten years, and most frighteningly, my bishop. As an ordained United Methodist minister, I was under full-time appointment by the bishop, splitting my work load between a local congregation and what had officially become a United Methodist-related counseling center only two years earlier. On top of all that, there was the twenty-member Conference Board of Ordained Ministry to which I was professionally accountable *and* on which I served as a voting member. As you know from the introduction, disclosure also came in the middle of my term as president of the Jefferson City Ministerial Alliance. How did God want me to handle disclosure to the groups which were part of my life? What was I to say them, and would I have the courage to say it?

There's really not time in this book to share all that took place during the final three weeks of December, but I must tell you about the lowest point of all—the point when all my worst fears did become reality. It was December 30, and a heavy snow covered the ground as I drove onto the parking lot of the bishop's St. Louis office. We were meeting to discuss my rather generic letter of resignation from Russellville Church and my request for early retirement from the active ministry.

My disclosure experiences to date had been so positive that I suppose I naively expected that trend to continue uninterrupted. Such was not to be the case this day, however. When I began to share with the Bishop the actual reasons behind my pending divorce and desire for early retirement, I was stopped dead in my tracks by a church official who could not find the compassion in his heart to hear what I needed to say.

"So, what do you expect from me, DOCTOR Norman? Surely you know you've left me no alternative other than to take your credentials. The *Book of Discipline* is clear: Paragraph 402.2 states that 'homosexuality is incompatible with Christian teachings,' and that 'no self-avowed, practicing homosexual' is appointable within the United Methodist system. You shouldn't have told me this. You knew the consequences. I want you to surrender your orders, and I want you to do so today."

As I remember it, those words were not said with kindness. There was no conversation about my personal well-being, about the impact of all this on my family, or any inclination on the Bishop's part to "be my pastor."

As best I can recall, I remained remarkably calm in the midst of the Bishop's condemnation. I believe God had prepared me for that moment. Under the guidance of two of my seminary professors (one of whom wrote the preface to this book), I was prepared to defend the right to keep my credentials in order by early retirement. I had no intention of giving in to the Bishop's strict interpretation of the *Book of Discipline*.

It certainly wasn't my idea of fun to take on a bishop of the United Methodist Church. Yet I did have to defend myself, and after collecting my thoughts, I said something like "Bishop, I admit I'm gay, but I have no comment concerning my relational status with anyone, be they male or female. Whom I may love, and ways that love may express itself, is not the business of this Conference. What I'm saying is, I have no intention of identifying myself as a 'practicing' homosexual, whatever the church may mean by that term. And since there are no charges for misconduct pending against me, I believe I have the disciplinary right of early retirement."

A considerable conflict ensued, but the bishop was a strict adherent to the *Book of Discipline*, and he eventually conceded that my request was technically in order. Although I was forty-eight years old at the time, he insisted on calling me "young man," which I somehow took as a put-down. "Young man," he said, "I'll grant your early retirement, but there are a few conditions. You are to say nothing publicly about your orientation until after annual Conference in June, you are to say nothing about it in your retirement address at the Seat of Conference itself, and you are not to return to Russellville Church from this day forward. You are through there. Your superintendent will cover the pulpit until a replacement is named. I won't have you subjecting those fine people to ... well .... You're through there. That's all."

And the Bishop was through with me, too. I was dismissed from his office and never spoke to the man directly again. When the retirement ceremony came some five months later, the Bishop shook my hand on the Conference platform, but looked through me as if I didn't exist.

Long before that retirement ceremony though, I learned that even if I could not depend upon the ecclesiastical leadership of my church for support, there was a segment of the church upon whom I could depend. My close friends in the Russellville congregation weren't about to pretend as if I didn't exist! When I was restricted by the hierarchy from going to them, many of them came to me. Cards, letters, visits to my counseling office, invitations to lunch and dinner—I was amazed.

After ten years of working together, of trusting and loving one another, of baptizing the newborn and burying the dead, my real friends weren't about to be told how to feel by a bishop who had never set foot inside their building. I still have numerous relationships within the Russellville congregation, and for that matter, in the community at large.

I've been told by friends of course, that the gossip mill ran non-stop following my resignation from the Russellville pulpit. Apparently, many individuals initially felt betrayed and extremely angry, shocked beyond belief that I would separate from my family for any reason, let alone this one!

As the cold months of winter gradually gave way to spring, the secret that the Bishop wanted kept increasingly became a matter of public knowledge— that "Dr. Norman was gay," and moreover, that he "had a boyfriend" with whom he was actually living in Kansas City! Needless to say, all that stretched the concept of non-judgmental Christian love to the max!

I'm sure that most of the people who knew me had little or no real understanding of what I'd done or why I had done it, and I'm absolutely *certain* most didn't approve of "homosexuality." Yet they somehow seemed to go on approving of me, gay or not. I know this may be very difficult for you to believe, but I was not subjected to a single negative experience by either the wonderful people of the Russellville congregation or the community at large. As the months passed, even many of those who thought my behavior was "sick" or "immoral," found ways to express their continued acceptance and love of me as a person.

There were some persons, of course, who were not so charitable in their assessment of the direction my life had taken, individuals who apparently wanted nothing to do with an openly gay man. But even those individuals kept their distance, and when our paths did cross, they treated me with dignity and respect. I want to say again, I was not subjected to a single negative experience by the wonderful people of the Russellville community.

As amazing as my parishioners and the community proved to be, no less amazing were my clients at the counseling center in Jefferson City. One by one, I came out to them in the privacy of individual sessions, explaining that I had separated from my wife of twenty years and why. To my astonishment, one by one they recovered from their initial shock, shrugged their shoulders, and went on with their own stories.

I had always assumed that coming out would bring my counseling practice in central Missouri to a halt. Instead, the clients I had been seeing continued to come to sessions, and new referrals kept coming. The truth of the matter is, I continued to see clients in Jefferson City regularly for three full years after publicly disclosing my gay orientation.

So what can I tell you? Virtually all my preconceptions concerning coming out publicly were shattered as a now "openly gay Rev. Dr. Norman" continued to be accepted by the community in which he had lived and worked for over two decades. All this leads me to an axiom which seems remarkably dependable: *Individuals who know us personally tend to accept us at the same level of our own self-acceptance.*

It's pretty amazing to realize that all this took place in middle America, at the geographic center of a conservative state where sodomy laws remain part of the criminal code. I ask myself constantly the extent to which my story really applies to others, the extent to which other families in other parts of the country can expect to be embraced the way my family was embraced. After all, there are still social norms and powerful institutional structures which not only perpetrate homophobia, but also restrict the freedom of persons caught within these structures from expressing public compassion towards persons of same gender orientation.

A good example of such institutional entrapment may have been the situation faced by my Bishop. The fact is, I have no knowledge of what he personally thought or felt about me. I only know how he behaved, given the institution in which he functioned. Regardless of what his personal sentiments may have been, he was trapped within a structure which compelled him to take the position he took. The United Methodist Church required that he "do his duty," even if doing so brought pain to him personally.

I suspect corporate executives, educational administrators, government officials, military officers, even middle-level managers in small businesses, are confronted with similar dilemmas regularly. What I am suggesting is this: Not everyone who stands against same-gender oriented individuals *publicly*, necessarily stands against them *privately*. Perhaps, just perhaps, things are not always as they appear on the surface.

I suppose we should now re-ask the question, "What possible good can come from voluntary disclosure?" What more do you need to know in order to draw your own conclusion as to the answer? Undoubtedly, you need to know what has happened with my wife and our children, and me personally the past seven years. I will try to relate that information as briefly as possible.

After two more years of on-going struggle and pain, Mary and I divorced in the spring of 1993. Since that time our communication skills have improved considerably, and as a result, I believe we understand and appreciate one another more genuinely than ever before. The relationship which has emerged is characterized by a deep level of mutual concern, but also by the reality of having "let go," each freeing the other to go on with life.

Mary entered the profession of social work and has remarried. She says she is doing well, and I believe she is happy.

David went on to graduate from high school and entered Westminster College in the fall of 1991. After a successful year there, he decided his future was on the Colorado ski slopes. I was proud David had the courage to act upon his dream and not wait half a lifetime to do what was right for the person he felt himself to be. He remains there today, working in a ski shop in season and doing construction during the summer months. His spare time is absorbed by rock climbing—much to the horror of those of us who watch him go straight up the side of a mountain. No, David hasn't thus far lived out the life script others might have willed for him. He's done something far more difficult: He's written his own script and watched it become reality.

And Annika? She went on to become both winter sports and prom queen during her senior year, and in May of 1993 graduated valedictorian of a class of 600. In the fall of that year she moved to Kansas City and entered Rockhurst, a Jesuit college only a few blocks from my office. As this book goes to press, she is engaged to a wonderful young man and is completing her first year of medical school at the University of Missouri in Columbia.

Thomas, meanwhile, lives with his mother and stepfather. He's an honor roll student who seems legitimately interested in all the things a parent would hope a fifteen-year-old would care about. Like his grandfather Norman, he loves basketball and spends every free moment on the court. He's determined to play college ball and then go on to be drafted by an NBA team.

Should I discourage Tom's dreams? Some would say "yes," pointing out that "such an achievement is against all statistical odds." But given what has happened to me and the people I love over the past few years, I believe in dreams and in the reality which they have the potential to create. No, I'll do all I can to encourage Tom. Who knows, perhaps one day I'll sit in my own living room and watch him play in a nationally televised game.

And then there's me, of course. What have the past seven years brought to pass in my life? I moved to

Kansas City in January of 1991 and opened a practice where I began specializing in issues related to gender orientation. A rough couple of years followed as I worked to get that new practice up and going. Southwestern Bell initially refused to allow Yellow Page advertising of my intended specialization—*Counseling for Gay Men, Lesbians & Bisexuals, Their Families & Friends*. They found the words "offensive" and "out of step with community values." Fairness eventually prevailed however, and I was allowed to word an ad clearly setting forth the nature of my practice. Meanwhile, most of my professional colleagues continued to insist that limiting myself to such a practice would never work, that I would "never make a living with it in Kansas City."

The only good part of the slow start was the fact that it allowed me to return to Jefferson City three days a week and continue seeing my clients there. I hated the one-hundred-fifty-mile commute, but it provided opportunity to phase out that practice over a period of time *and* to see all three of my children on a weekly basis. All things considered, life found a way to work itself out, and by the spring of 1994 I was able to close the Jefferson City office and focus all of my energy working with issues related to gender orientation.

The transition brought with it near financial ruin, and I still struggle to stay one step ahead of the bill collectors. But I'm doing what I want, what I know deep in my soul God has called me to do, and with that realization comes a level of peace and well-being that I've never known before.

The practice has flourished, and other counselors have joined the office through the years. I myself have gone on to further limit my own practice to *Therapy for Gay Married Men, Their Wives and Families.* Others have joked that such a limited specialization may put me in "a group of one, nationally." Whatever the case may be, I enjoy my work with individuals struggling through orientational transition and the opportunity to bring such persons together for group therapy. Needless to say, this book is a direct outgrowth of that work.

I need to tell you, too, that most of what God has helped me achieve would not have been possible had it not been for a man named Jeff. We met in the fall of 1990 and established a home together after my move to Kansas City several months later. The new practice itself was born of our common dream, and Jeff worked beside me as office manager daily for over five years.

Entering into a committed, gender-appropriate relationship was a new experience for both of us. Never before had life offered an opportunity for such authenticity. But let me tell you, making that relationship work wasn't easy! We were both programmed in childhood by a heterosexual script which instilled in us the belief that "gay relationships never really work long term," that they are "a perversion of natural order," and "not genuine love at all." The truth is, we've struggled long and hard to defy the odds which have attempted to separate us. We've been determined not to allow internalized homophobia to sabotage our love for one another. Even though physical separation did come to pass after five years together, Jeff's move to Florida was a mutual decision, one made with the full intention of freeing one another for continued growth.

What more should I say? Well, letting go has been hard, but Jeff and I are gradually building a genuine friendship in which we continue to experience mutual love each for the other. We maintain regular contact by phone and mail, and do all we can to support one another emotionally as God leads our futures.

Perhaps most amazing of all, is what has happened to me physically as a result of orientational authenticity. Gradually the pounds melted away as normal eating to sustain life replaced my addictive relationship with food. Alcohol consumption ceased to be a problem as moderate social drinking replaced my late night binges with a six-pack. Thankfully, I was not physiologically addicted to alcohol after all; and as I no longer had feelings from which I needed to escape, I no longer needed an agent to achieve that escape.

Even my life-long work addiction began to give way to a reasonable life-style, affording me opportunities for regular exercise and times away for rest and relaxation. As I write the very words you are reading, I have taken a few days off to help my friend, Constance Wise (who, by the way, is the editor of this book) move to Denver where she's entering a Ph.D. program in theology.

As I bring this chapter to a close, I'm sitting here in Pete's Grill, adjacent to the University of Denver campus, dressed in a blue pullover and a pair of thirty-three-inch Levi's jeans. My weight is an ideal one hundred-sixty pounds and before the day is over I'll hit the gym for my every-other-day workout. I'm thankful to God to report that I've returned to excellent physical health and have not needed prescribed medications in over five years.

What I'm suggesting is this: God's continual insistence on orientational authenticity saved me just before work, and food, and alcohol addictions took my life! So what possible good came from voluntary disclosure in my case? I'm alive, and this summer I'll be there to walk my daughter down the aisle on the occasion of her marriage. I'm saying that without disclosure there would have been no authenticity, and without authenticity, I believe I would by now be dead.

With all my heart, I believe that disclosure really was the passageway to authenticity—with its precious gifts of spiritual, emotional, and physical well-being—and that all of us have benefited from living a life of truth.

Conclusion

After four and a half years of daily work to write the book you've just read, I find it difficult to realize that all that remains is the conclusion. The journey through this process has taken me time and again down dead-end streets as my own defense mechanisms attempted to delay discovery of truth. At other times God led me to new insight more quickly than my conscious mind could apprehend. The journey has been characterized by times of fear and anger, times of depression, times of extreme personal pain, all interspersed with moments of great joy.

I want you to know as this work comes to a close that it has been the most rewarding venture of my life. In spite of the energy it has consumed and the uncertainty it has created, I have no regrets and would do it all again. I'm even glad that modern technology makes it possible for me to self-publish what I have written, rather than sell the manuscript to a commercial publisher. By maintaining all rights to my work, I can revise the text and reissue the book as my own evolutionary process provides new insight.

Only now in preparing this conclusion, for example, have I realized that my own discovery and disclosure process fell into four seven-year periods spanning nearly three decades. During courtship and the first five years of marriage, my orientational repression was so complete that I had little or no conscious recognition of my true gay orientation. Then came the second seven-year period during which the process gradually enabled me to experience myself as bisexual, a realization which I suppressed the vast majority of the time. And I shudder to remember the third seven-year period after repression lifted and I became fully aware of my true gay orientation, a period during which addiction almost took my life. Finally, with disclosure came the birth of the current period of orientational authenticity with its gifts of spiritual, emotional, and physical well-being.

I'm not yet sure what new truth will emerge for me in the years ahead, but I've learned to trust the process and the God who leads me through it. It is clear that one of the claims of God on my life will be to continue to do research and to write in the area of orientational transition. I envision at least two more books—one dealing with the specific questions wives, children, and parents ask when gay married men come out, and one addressed to gay married men themselves.

If your family is going through orientational transition, I hope the revelation of the Norman family journey will both enlighten and shorten your own evolutionary process, that it will lessen the pain and enhance the love which you and your family experience. Lest I fail to make the point in all these words, let me say again that the guiding principle is *just tell the truth*. As I said in Chapter Two, the truth is often frightening, yet it literally has the power to save our lives. Truth heals individuals and sick relationships. It has the potential to displace isolation and loneliness with authentic intimacy. It liberates us from the secrets and deceptions of the past. It sets us free to embrace the potentials of the future. It is the energy, the life-force of new being. My single most important goal in undertaking the authorship of this book has been to persuade you to embrace the power of truth and allow it to transform your future.

Fortunately, we in America now live in a society increasingly open to truth concerning same gender orientation. Who would have thought even two years ago that Americans would be watching and laughing at sitcoms such as "Ellen," and making box office hits of movies such as "Bird Cage," "My Best Friend's Wedding," or "In and Out"? Yes, it's hard to imagine that the closing years of the twentieth century would bring such openness and social affirmation of gay men and lesbians. Things are changing. Obviously our society is learning to laugh at situations involving same gender orientation and to see it for what it is—a normal part of everyday life. I suspect our changing social climate will make the journey you and your family must take considerably easier than the one experienced by the Norman family.

This new openness is not limited to TV and the movies. Mental health professionals and church leaders have begun to affirm the normalcy of same gender orientation. Earlier you read of the ground-breaking positions taken by the American Psychological Association and the American Council of Bishops of the Roman Catholic Church. These two very different organizations have concluded that same gender orientation is neither a mental nor a spiritual disorder.

Other groups are bringing us the same message. Today in most metropolitan areas there are congregations of mainline Protestant denominations which have made the decision to affirm same gender orientation and to reach out to gay men, lesbians, and their families. In the United Methodist Church they are called Reconciling Congregations, and part of their ministry is to welcome all persons into full membership and participation in church life, regardless of gender orientation. Also, virtually every major city in America has a chapter of PFLAG (Parents and Friends of Lesbians and Gays). Made up primarily of heterosexual members, PFLAG has an impressive array of programs and services to support individuals and families struggling with issues related to same gender orientation.

The existence of such organizations is of little or no help if you isolate yourself, however. I encourage you not to do that. As soon as you feel able, reach out to a gay-affirmative congregation or a local chapter of PFLAG. Draw support from such groups and lend your support to them. Affiliate yourself with those organizations which have the courage to stand against homophobia in all its forms, and which affirm that gay individuals have the same right as all other Americans to full acceptance in our great society. As you join in the movement calling for social equality without regard to gender orientation, I believe your own life will be enriched.

Also, I encourage you to reach out to trusted family members and friends. Tell them what's going on. You need their understanding and support as you work through the difficult transition ahead. I believe you will be amazed at the genuine love and acceptance which most will gladly offer. The fact is, though, they can't help if they don't know what you are facing. Trust others with the truth, then accept their support.

You may want to seek out a gay-affirmative therapist for a while, preferably one who is experienced in working with families going through orientational transition. Don't be afraid to ask if they support the position of the American Psychological Association concerning the normalcy of same gender orientation. If they don't, or if their answer is ambiguous, cancel the appointment and look for a therapist who is clearly in step with the position now taken by the vast majority of mental health professionals.

And, of course, there are those things you can do which are strictly private. I'm speaking of reading good books and keeping up with current affairs concerning gender orientation. I am saying you can educate yourself. You can get the facts, then personally decide what action life calls you to take.

As you seek to educate yourself, I encourage you to become familiar with the work of the Norman Institute here in Kansas City. It was founded as a nonprofit educational corporation in the fall of 1997, and focuses exclusively on issues related to gender orientation. The Institute's mission is to add momentum to the shift in global consciousness toward societal acceptance of orientational diversity. In pursuit of its mission, the Institute focuses on two primary objectives: 1) the discovery and dissemination of factual information concerning gender orientation; and, 2) the healing of individuals and families struggling with gay, lesbian, bisexual, or transgender issues.

While the Institute is affiliated with no church or religious organization, it was the conviction of founding board members that the journey toward orientational authenticity needs to be understood as a spiritual process. That is to say, it is God who calls persons to live congruently, and the affirmation of one's true gender orientation is an act of compliance with the divine lure toward well-being.

You can keep up with the Institute's work by accessing its homepage on the World Wide Web at www.NormanInstitute.org. You will find there an on-line bookstore which offers next-day shipping of all titles in stock, a Website magazine dedicated to keeping readers informed on current issues concerning gender orientation, and the "help lines"—a resource directory designed to help individuals locate information specifically related to the dilemma they face.

The Website magazine includes a regular column written by me, in which I answer questions submitted directly by readers. Eventually, the magazine will even provide an opportunity for readers to share their own success stories through the remarkable technology of the World Wide Web.

If you don't have a computer at home with access to the Internet, remember that the service is free at most local libraries. If you are unsure how to get onto the net or find a particular Website, ask the librarian for assistance. Once you're familiar with the access procedures, the full services of the Institute will be at your fingertips thereafter.

If you have comments or suggestions about the work of the Institute, or would like to share with me personally your own story, I invite you to write me in care of the Norman Institute, P.O. Box 45600, Kansas City, Missouri, 64171. Much remains to be learned about how families are handling orientational transition and I welcome any response you care to make.

§§§

Before bringing this conclusion to a close, let's turn one last time to you and ask how all this applies to your family. If someone you love has thrust your family into orientational transition, you know the fear and anger, depression, and extreme personal pain I described in my story. And you are wondering if you will ever experience the moments of joy.

Yes, some of the emotions will be the same, but your journey is your own because it is happening to your family. The details of what you experience as the gay married man you love discovers his true gender orientation will arise from your family history and will reflect your family's values, as well as the interpersonal dynamics of your family relationships. Let it be your own story. Let it unfold naturally, always remembering that this difficult transition is a process. It will take time. Try to be patient with yourself, with others in your family, and with the gay married man you love.

Let us not be naive, however: There will be moments when your patience will be tested to the max. Although we as Americans are learning to accept gay individuals, homophobia is still alive and well in much of our society. As you learn to accept the truth about the gay man you love, you will encounter some individuals and institutions who cannot yet be as accepting. Sometimes their judgmentalism arises from their own fear and pain—their homophobia. In other cases individuals are caught in rigid institutions with regulations which do not allow them to be more kind.

As much as possible, take all this into consideration as you make your response, and try not to let them get to you.

Far more important, however, than the criticism of those few who find they need to be negative, will be the amazing support you will receive from the many family members and friends who will continue to love you throughout this difficult transition. As you share your dilemma openly and honestly, realizing that it is God who is trying to lead the man you love and his family into full authenticity, others will tend to take your lead and respond in kind. I really believe you will find the axiom I stated in Chapter 19 amazingly true. As you share your story, you will find that *individuals who have known and loved your family prior to the onset of the coming out process, will tend to accept you at the same level of your own self-acceptance.* So try to be non-apologetic and self-affirming. It gives others permission to do likewise.

What I'm saying is that the situation you face will tend to become exactly what you make it. Attitude is everything here. If you see disclosure as the end of the world, it will tend to become exactly that—a death sentence. But you do have a choice. You can see the coming out process as an opportunity for a new beginning, as an opportunity to allow openness and honesty to lead you and your family to authenticity.

As you move through this difficult transition, I urge you again to reach out to a congregation that welcomes gay and lesbian members, to such organizations as PFLAG, to loving family members and friends, and to consider at least a few professional counseling sessions with a gay-affirmative therapist.

However, the greatest resource of all is actually within you! Whether recognized and affirmed consciously or not, God is within each person and each moment in time, doing all that God can to lift orientational repression and bring about maximum well-being for everyone involved.

I'm saying there is a divine ally at the very core of your soul who loves you and loves the gay married man you love. With all my heart, I believe that God will help you embrace the truth and lead you and your family toward authenticity, with its precious gifts of spiritual, emotional, and physical well-being.

Terry Norman
Kansas City, Mo.
New Year's Day 1998

Appendix A
On Orientational Repression

The concept of *Orientational Repression* is a postulation arising from my own life experiences. I know it explains what I personally went through as a gay male, and I believe it accurately describes the life journey of most gay men who dutifully marry in their late teens or twenties. It should be noted, however, that the construct may be somewhat less descriptive of gay males entering heterosexual marriage in the more socially liberal closing decades of the twentieth century.

The process leading to orientational repression begins long before puberty, when young boys find themselves drawn far more to other boys than to girls, and in a way they intrinsically know is "different" from the natural curiosity of their peers. Realizing their feelings and desires are socially unacceptable, they are driven by fear to hide those feelings, even from themselves.

The process of denial is insidious, and full repression of their desire *to love and be loved by another man* occurs across decades, rather than resulting from a single traumatic event. Ever so gradually, they know less and less of themselves, as congruence increasingly defers to the pressure for social compliance. Ever so gradually, all that remains in conscious awareness is a limited knowledge of *sexual interest* in persons of their own gender. Convincing themselves that such sexual interest has nothing to do with love, they successfully suppress even those emotions most of the time, believing that all attraction to other men will cease to exist once they are happily married.

Somewhere in the late teens or twenties the process is complete, and the orientationally repressed gay male is ready for heterosexual marriage. Stated differently, he is ready for the pseudo-heterosexualism of orientationally repressed adulthood. In regard to same gender orientation, I am convinced the goal of the superego is no less than the absolute death of the ego, the total capitulation of one's true self to the parental and social forces of upbringing. I believe the entry of a gay male into heterosexual marriage is best understood as just such a death—the death of orientational authenticity at the hand of a relentless and powerful superego, one which demands absolute compliance with the heterosexual norm.

I don't think I would have ever realized the process I myself went through had I not undertaken authorship of this book. Coming to see how repressed adulthood—and orientational repression in particular—characterized my life has been a long and difficult road. I'm certain I have described the process accurately, but there was a time I could not have been convinced that such a phenomenon even existed. In those days I saw myself as a strong, self-determining individual who could accomplish anything I set out to do. In reality, however, most of the major decisions of life—including marriage—were made under the influence of a superego so strong as to render my true self all but non-existent. It's humbling to plead "diminished capacity," to admit that my true self had so little say in what actually came to pass in the early decades of life; yet such was the case. Moreover, I believe it is the case for virtually all gay men who dutifully marry at the socially appointed time.

Appendix B
On Polymorphous Pansexuality and the Gay Married Male

I have come to believe the ability of gay men to function sexually within heterosexual marriages is a manifestation of *Homo sapiens'* polymorphous pansexual nature. My formulation of this hypothesis has grown out of the observation by Freud and others that human sexual *behavior* can take many forms; that by potential at least, it is "all inclusive." To the best of my knowledge, the term *polymorphous pansexuality* was first used in the early 1900s to describe the sexual behavior of certain severely regressed psychiatric patients who appeared to respond and function sexually to any stimuli available. Such a construct suggests that sexual libido—the id's instinctual drive for sexual satisfaction—is actually gender-neutral, and that it is capable of expressing itself in a wide variety of ways as directed internally by either the ego or superego, or externally by environmental conditions.

If such is actually the case, that means the human is theoretically capable of exclusively heterosexual *behavior*, bisexual *behavior*, or exclusively homosexual *behavior*, depending on his mental state and/or environmental circumstance. It also means that Kinsey was correct in reporting that human sexual behavior lies along a continuum characterized by the exact same potentialities. In other words, we humans beings appear physiologically capable of adapting to whatever pattern of sexual behavior life mandates, and that includes behaving in ways incongruent with one's true gender orientation, or abstaining from sexual behavior altogether.

Now, how does all this specifically apply to gay men who enter heterosexual marriage? I am suggesting that gay men adapt to heterosexual behavior in marriage the same way many straight men adapt to homosexual behavior in prison, and the same way many regressed psychiatric patients adapt to indiscriminate bisexual behavior during periods of hospitalization—by denying their authentic ego-based emotions with regard to gender orientation and performing sexually in whatever way the circumstance permits or demands.

For gay men who eventually marry, such denial on a sustained basis typically leads to outright orientational repression. That is to say, they become consciously *unaware* of their need to love and be loved by another man, functioning sexually with their heterosexual spouse as if straight. Stated differently, when the ego becomes inert with regard to one's true orientation, libido is inevitably directed by the heterosexual script of the superego, resulting in mechanical, robotic sexual relations with the opposite gender, but in ways devoid of present-centered, authentic emotion.

If all this sounds a lot like abuse, it's because that's exactly the right word! It is abuse, of both gay men and the women they marry. And just as the survivors of incest and rape tend to repress the emotions associated with the pain they suffered, gay men tend to repress systematically the emotions associated with the very sexual intimacy in which they physically participate.

I first became aware of this startling phenomenon only in the summer of 1996 as I worked my way through the final manuscript of this book. I discovered that I myself had little recall of the sexually intimate details of my own marriage, and virtually none of my wedding night itself! Shocked, I spent weeks intentionally regressing to the occasion of my marriage, just "trying to remember," only to discover that the memory traces were simply not there.

Finally accepting the fact that I had repressed virtually all such memory, I set out to interview as many gay married men as possible. I needed to know if my experience was unique, or if others repressed such memory as well. I know this is hard to believe and that my findings will be viewed with great suspicion, but *none* of the gay married men I have interviewed thus far has any substantial recall of the sexually intimate details of his own honeymoon! It is as if he were not there; yet each recalls in vivid detail his first sexual experience with another man.

What we have here, I believe, is a repressed memory syndrome of which mental health professionals have not been aware. And what happens when such repression begins to lift, when gradually evolving orientational authenticity brings the gay husband to conscious awareness of his life-long need to love and be loved by another man? He gradually loses interest in behaving heterosexually in bed. To do so now requires either complete emotional detachment or the engagement in a private fantasy of gender appropriate nature.

Moreover, it appears that the vast majority of gay married men find even those emotional strategies run their course. They become increasingly impotent with their wives, and sexual expression within the marriage relationship becomes a thing of the past.

Much research remains to be done into this whole phenomenon, and certainly my informal findings will need to be verified by carefully designed clinical research. Nevertheless, I feel confident what I have presented here is accurate and that the future will yield valuable insights into a complex aspect of personality about which we've historically had little information.

Appendix C
On Spirituality, and the Evolution of Orientational Authenticity

Is there an order, a progressive sequence, through which gay married men move as orientational repression begins to lift? I believe there is, and my clinical experience with an increasingly large number of such persons has led to the following hypothesis: Once gay married men begin to recognize their true orientation, there appear to be four developmental stages through which mentally healthy individuals progress as orientational authenticity evolves. They are: 1) the sexual exploration stage; 2) the intimate relationship stage; 3) the community affiliation stage; and 4) the spiritual integration stage.

In Chapter 15 I have characterized each of the first three stages in considerable detail. As I've shared this information with my more highly evolved gay married clients, I have found that virtually all recognize themselves in each stage immediately. On one particular occasion in the spring of 1997, I read the draft of what was to become Chapter 15 to a therapy group of six gay married men. When I finished, one individual said with a laugh, "Well, that's my life alright! How did you know?"

It was no joke. As the group discussed what they had just heard, each member agreed that they were thoroughly familiar with the feelings and behaviors of what I had called stages one, two and three. With only minor exceptions, they agreed that the hypothesis captured the very essence of the life they had lived.

Until they heard them delineated, however, the individuals who made up that therapy group had little awareness that such stages even existed. It was as if they recognized the process through which they had moved only in retrospect, and only when pointed out.

It was the consensus of the group that each stage had first been experienced in a linear, sequential order, but that the stages tended to run concurrently for an extended period of time thereafter. Most members felt they had vacillated continuously from one stage to another as orientational authenticity slowly evolved. Some felt they were still vacillating.

Regardless of the order in which the stages are experienced or how long they last, this much seems clear—gay married men have underlying needs which drive the behaviors of each stage, and only as those needs are met are they free to move on with the developmental process.

I believe the stages of which we have spoken thus far are easily verified by the observational techniques of behavioral science, and that we will eventually understand the needs associated with each stage. Consensus among mental health practitioners with access to gay married men should come easily, given the essentially self-evident nature of each stage. One wonders, in fact, why such an obvious and seemingly universal process remained so obscure for so long.

Similar consensus will not be easily achieved, however, in regard to what I have chosen to call the Spiritual Integration Stage. If you have read Chapter 15, you already know that I included only one lone paragraph concerning Stage Four. It reads: The *Spiritual Integration Stage* is without doubt the least recognized, but ultimately the most important stage of all. In this stage gay men come to experience their orientation as a God-given, sacred blessing. Gripped by divine love, gay men experience the shame and guilt of internalized homophobia gradually giving way to genuine self-acceptance. Joy replaces depression and life takes on new meaning. It becomes increasingly important to treat both themselves and others with dignity and respect. All things seem to be dramatically transformed as love becomes a way of life, and most striking of all is the transformation from self-contempt to authentic self-love. It is at this point, I believe, when orientational authenticity can be called "mature," or "fully evolved."

I want you to know that I had only limited awareness of what I've come to call the *Spiritual Integration Stage* until long after the process had transformed my life. Only in retrospect have I come to realize that God has always been at the core of my soul, doing for me constantly what I could not do for myself. God not only gave me life, he has been about the business of saving it time and again! I believe it was God who led me into orientational repression to save me physically when I became too emotionally frail to survive otherwise; then out of repression and into congruent living once my family and I had the ego-strength to face the truth. I'm saying the naming and claiming of my same gender orientation was an act of divine grace, a sacred moment of new birth, and I believe Mary, the children, and I have all benefited from the authenticity it brought.

Like myself, most gay married men fail to sense the motivating source behind their discovery and disclosure process until long after it has transformed their lives. Only in retrospect, it seems, do they come to realize that the journey toward orientational authenticity was a spiritual process.

It's crucial to make clear that the spirituality of which I speak is about our journey inward and about communion with the God experienced there. It is about the journey into one's own soul—that aspect of the psyche where we are all one with the creative source of life.

What a remarkably different process that is from learning of God through the doctrines and creeds of organized religion. What an awesome thing it is, to apprehend divine truth as it arises from one's own soul, rather than searching for it in the traditions and rituals external to the self. To experience the holy as intrinsic to our very being is exciting indeed, and to celebrate the communion from which ultimate authority arises almost defies verbal description.

And what a different outcome we gay men experience, based on where we seek the holy: In organized religion external to ourselves, we find almost universal condemnation; at the core of our soul, where we are one with the holy, we find unconditional love. It is there, at the core of our being where we know we are known by the God who created us, that we experience the ultimate affirmation of a divine "yes!"

The truth is, many of us are driven inward for comfort and peace as a result of the harsh judgmentalism of those who purport to speak for God. And what a surprise it is, to find there a God who stands in opposition to those who pronounce such judgments.

I believe God longs to pull us all inward toward himself, that he creates an inner vacuum that draws us toward the holy. I believe God waits there, longing to become one with our conscious reality, longing to assure us of his love, and above all else, longing to lead our lives toward authenticity—with its precious gifts of spiritual, emotional, and physical well-being.

§ § §

Many individuals undoubtedly will deny the very existence of what I have called the *Spiritual Integration Stage*, refusing to believe that "God" or "spirituality" have anything to do with the evolution of orientational authenticity. Moreover, they will undoubtedly claim—and correctly so—that such an assertion moves us from psychology to the realm of philosophical theology.

I acknowledge that what you are reading in this appendix is a faith statement on my part, a credo that has evolved from the experience of God in both myself and others. As such, the postulations concerning a *Spiritual Integration Stage* can be neither proven nor invalidated by empirical scientific methods. What I have written here is simply what I hold to be true, what has arisen to consciousness from the depths of my own soul. I believe the very essence of such "knowing" is a matter of intrinsic wisdom, an experience of the holy from within, not the recitation of knowledge from some extrinsic source.

I would like you to know that the positions taken in this book, and particularly in this appendix, are grounded solidly in the process philosophy of Alfred North Whitehead and the great theologians who have followed his lead. Process theology has proven so important to my understanding of orientational authenticity that I shall take what few pages remain and discuss briefly it's basic principals.

I believe that process theology is best understood as the evolutionary theology of our modern era, a theology that is evolving today even as we live and speak, even as you read the very words printed on these pages. It is an understanding of God that breathes with the moment, which takes its life from the experience of our very being. Process theology is grounded not in what others have said in the past, but what God says from the depths of our own souls in the moment. It is a theology moving in sync with the evolving world, one which attempts to explain what is taking place both within and around us at each moment in time.

The God of this evolving order is universal in nature, of course, having been known in mosques, synagogues and temples, sanctuaries and around tribal campfires since time immemorial. The God of process has been called by many names and understood in many ways across the course of human history, all relevant to the people for the time in which they lived. This God refuses to be the exclusive property of any people, of any dogma, at any time in history. Rather, this God is the source behind the ingenious creative spirit of them all. I believe process thought parallels the scientific world's understanding of the evolving nature of all physical life. Accordingly, it holds that virtually nothing remains unchanged across time, including God himself.

Although it varies dramatically from traditional thinking, let us be clear that the creative source which process theology calls "God" is pure spirit in nature, not restricted to physical form or gender characteristics (my frequent reference to God as if physical in form and male in gender not withstanding).

The God of process is ultimately a very imminent God, one who resides not transcendently on some other side of the universe, but at the core of our very being. This inseparable relatedness occurs with or without our knowledge and consent, just as it occurs between homo sapiens and lesser evolved forms of life. And such relatedness extends to Mother Earth herself, the support system for all living things.

From God's primordial nature, the creative source of the universe envisions the best possible potential for the moment we are about to live. Moreover, God does all God can to help us grasp that potential as the moment takes birth. I'm saying, the initial aim of God is *always* there, attempting to lead both us and the world toward well-being.

And the God of process is no passive bystander who looks on disinterestedly as we attempt to actualize that initial aim. Rather, God co-experiences with us its actualization as a consequence of inseparable relatedness to all things. Through God's consequential nature, the creator of the universe feels the joy of our achievements and the pain of our failures. Yes, the God of process is a very personal God indeed; one who experiences the full emotionality of our being, a divine ally who stands with us at each moment in time.

Let's look now at process theology's use of the term "prehension." It's crucial that we understand this concept. As each new moment of existence prepares to unfold, all that has been in our past attempts to influence what is about to be. In other words, our past wants to replicate itself. Simultaneous with that urge to replicate, however, co-exists the initial aim of God for the absolute novel, the absolute new, the best of all possibilities for the occasion at hand. So, "to prehend" is to experience not only the collective impact of one's past, but also the God who is attempting to lead the future. We need to understand, however, that awareness of such prehension is a late phase of consciousness, and unfortunately, most of what we humans prehend of the holy is never recognized as such.

In my doctoral dissertation 15 years ago, I hypothesized that a positive correlation existed between being open to ourselves emotionally and our ability to prehend the divine spirit at a conscious level. Even more so today, I believe the more open we are to ourselves and the more congruently we live, the more likely it is that the divine spirit will be prehended at a level of conscious awareness.

Whether or not we prehend God consciously, the creative spirit of the universe is there never-the-less, struggling to free us from the status quo, to bring about true novelty and change. In a process universe we are free to become what we have not been. We are determined not only by the influence of our individual and collective past, but also by a God who lures us into a new future.

Sounds pretty good doesn't it, the idea of a loving God giving an initial aim most appropriate for each moment in time, leading us ever onward toward an increasingly perfect world? But let's face it, life in this world is often no utopia, in spite of God's continual effort to lead us toward well-being. Genuine evil exists all around us, both moral and natural—that which, all things considered, we would have been better off without.

Philosophical and theological discourse throughout history, however, has tended to deny the existence of genuine evil, maintaining that what we consider evil only *appears* to be that way, that the sovereign God of the universe has "his" reasons for all that occurs, and that eventually we'll understand the good which *apparent evil* created.

Therein, perhaps, lies the most basic difference between process theology and most other philosophical and theological systems of thought. Process thinkers like myself maintain that the God of process leads this world not through coercive force, but by divine lure. Process thought holds, in fact, that God is in an on-going struggle against all forms of evil, doing all God can to maximize good at every point in time. But God has no monopoly on power. Far too often evil wins the battle temporarily, and good people suffer in the process.

God is with us in that suffering, however, and we can take comfort in knowing that such pain is never his will. Moreover, we can rest assured that the God of process will be there beyond the moment of our agony, helping us grow from the experience as we are lured endlessly toward life in a new tomorrow.

§ § §

I know some of what you just read may be difficult both to understand and accept, given its dramatic departure from the Judaic-Christian tradition as we have experienced it in America during the Twentieth Century. The concepts of process thought are often seen as abstract and all but incomprehensible. I believe, however, that God leads all of us to understand that which we are ready to understand, and that what may be somewhat unclear today, may be the very life-saving truth that becomes crystal clear tomorrow. As I think about my own tomorrow, I sense that the evolving process toward ever-increasing authenticity may well be leading me toward the authorship of a layman's guide to process thought. Who knows, God has his way with us in strange and mysterious ways.

Notes

1. Soren Kierkegaard in Ernest Becker, *The Denial of Death* (New York: The Free Press, 1973), 68.

2. John Money, *Gay, Straight & In-Between: The Sexology of Erotic Orientation* (New York: The Oxford University Press, 1988), 121 and 180.

3. To define orientation by sexual expression alone is to miss the point. Rather than being limited to mere sexual behavior, orientation involves the physical, emotional, and spiritual aspects of the whole person. Accordingly, I shall avoid linking the term "sexual" to "orientation."

4. Money, 11.

5. Money, 12.

6. "Always Our Children," Statement issued September 10, 1997, by the Office of Communications, National Conference of Catholic Bishops/United States Catholic Conference.

7. Money, 50.

8. Money, 50.

9. For a more complete discussion concerning the origin of same gender orientation, see Chandler Burr, *A Separate Creation: The Search for Biological Origins of Sexual Orientation* (New York: Hyperion, 1996).

10. Consistent with my upbringing, I have decided to speak of God in this book as if physical in form and masculine in gender, although I have come to perceive of the Holy as pure Spirit devoid of such characteristics. Moreover, I shall make every effort to speak of God in ways that do not limit our human experience of

the divine to the doctrines of any particular religion or theological school of thought.

11. When used in a theological context, the term "prehension" means to experience the collective impact of our past *and* the initial aim of God for the moment we are about to live. Even when not recognized consciously, God is always within the depth of our psyche, struggling to lure us toward the best possible potential for the occasion about to be. And always, the aim of God is designed to maximize well-being, both for us and the world in which we live. To the best of my knowledge, the term was first used this way in the process philosophy of Alfred North Whitehead in the 1930s. Such thought provides the theoretical construct around which I have come to understand my own life experience. The theories of process thought are reflected again and again in the pages of the very book you are now reading. For those of you who wish to explore process thought in greater detail, I would recommend John B. Cobb Jr. and David Ray Griffin, *Process Theology: An Introductory Exposition* (Philadelphia; The Westminster Press, 1976).

12. United Methodist Church, *The Book of Discipline* (Nashville: Cokesbury Press, 1972).

13. Joseph Nicolosi, *Reparative Therapy of Male Homosexuality: A New Clinical Approach* (Northvale, NJ: Jason Aronson Inc., 1991).

14. "Resolution on Appropriate Therapeutic Responses to Sexual Orientation," adopted by the American Psychological Association Council of Representatives, August 14, 1997.

15. Gregory M. Herek, "Attempts to Change Sexual Orientation." Copyright 1997. Available at: <http://psychology.ucdavis.edu/rainbow/html/facts_changing.html>.

16. Money, 12.

17. Paul Gibson, "Gay Male and Lesbian Youth Suicide" in Alcohol, Drug Abuse, and Mental Health Administration, Report on the Secretary's Task Force on Youth Suicide. Volume 3: Prevention and Interventions in Youth Suicide. DHHS Pub. No. (ADM)89-1623. Washington, D.C.: Supt. of Docs., U.S. Govt. Print. Off., 1989.

18. Missouri Department of Social Services, "Missouri Child Fatality Review Program for 1995." (December 1996).

19. Gary Remafedi, "Gay Male Youth Seven Times More Likely to report Suicide Attempts than Heterosexual Peers." Copyright 1997. Available at: <http://www.newswise.com/articles/GAYTEEN.UMN.html>.

20. Michael Shernoff, "So Many Drugs, So Little Time: When Recreation Becomes Dependence." *The New York Native*, February 1997. Available at: <http://mother.qrd.org/qrd/health/gay.men.and.recreational.drugs>.

21. Calvin S. Hall, *A Primer of Freudian Psychology* (New York, The New American Library, 1954) 58.

22. Vernon E. Johnson, *I'll Quit Tomorrow* (San Francisco, Harper & Row, 1980).

23. Stanley Siegal and Ed Lowe Jr., *Uncharted Lives: Understanding the Life Passages of Gay Men* (New York, Plume, 1995).

24. Mel White, *Stranger at the Gate: To be Gay and Christian in America* (New York: Simon & Schuster, 1994), 73.

25. Jean Schaar Gochros, *When Husbands Come Out of the Closet* (New York: Harrington Park Press, 1989).

26. Amity Pierce Buxton, *The Other Side of the Closet: The Coming-Out Crisis for Straight Spouses* (Santa Monica, CA: IBS Press, Inc., 1991).

27. Marshall Kirk and Hunter Madsen, *After the Ball: How America will Conquer its Fear and Hatred of Gays in the 90's* (New York: Plume, 1989), 18.

28. Karen Swann, "% Gay?" Bad Subjects, Issue #5, March/April 1993. Available at: <http://eng.hss.cmu.edu/bs/05/Swann.html>.

29. Donald H. Clark, *The New Loving Someone Gay* (Berkeley, CA; Celestial Arts, 1987).

30. Carl R. Rogers, *On Becoming a Person: A Therapist's View of Psychotherapy* (Boston; Houghton Mifflin Company, 1961).

norman institute
Wisdom for the Twenty-First Century

Dear Reader:

The Norman Institute is a nonprofit educational corporation focusing exclusively on issues related to gender orientation. In keeping with its mission of disseminating factual information, we are pleased to represent Dr. Norman as the promotional and distribution agent for *Just Tell the Truth*. The Board of Directors and I believe it offers the best answers available to the questions families ask when gay married men come out—answers simply not available elsewhere.

Copies of *Just Tell the Truth* may be obtained by calling our office at (816) 960-7200. If you prefer to order by mail, an order form follows this letter. All orders are processed within 24 hours and shipped in a priority mail envelope.

The Norman Institute also carries other books for immediate shipping which have been recommended by our reading committee. A list of those books is available from the Website, or may be obtained by writing the Norman Institute at PO Box 45600, Kansas City, Missouri 64171.

If you would like more information about the Norman Institute or its work, I invite you to contact our office. We are determined to do all we can to help individuals and families find the resources they need to live life authentically.

Eddie Miller,
Executive Director

$n\!i$ norman institute

(promotional and distribution agent for <u>Just Tell the Truth</u>)

Just Tell the Truth is about the thousands of gay men who enter heterosexual marriages, father children, and remain quietly in the closet until they voluntarily disclose their true gender orientation. Its purpose is to provide clear, concise answers to the questions families ask when gay married men come out. In a broader sense, however, this book should prove helpful to anyone seeking to understand the journey toward orientational authenticity.

Orders may be placed for next day shipping by:
Calling our office at (816) 960-7200
Or, by filling out the attached order form and returning it to:

Norman Institute Bookstore
P.O. Box 45600
Kansas City, Missouri 64171

- -

Order Form - *Just Tell the Truth*

Name: _____

Address: _____

City: _____ State: _____ Zip: _____

Phone: (_____)_____ (Necessary only with credit card orders)

Please send _____ book(s) @ $15.95 each
(Handling charge included) = _____

All orders shipped Priority Mail (1 to 4 day delivery):
Add $3.00 for 1-4 books; or $6.00 for 5-8 books + _____
(For discounts and shipping rates on quantity orders, call 816-960-7200)

ORDER TOTAL: $ _____

Payment Method: [ ] Money Order   [ ] Visa   [ ] Mastercard   [ ] Check

Credit Card Number: _____

Expiration Date: _____ Signature: _____

[ ] Please send me information about the Norman Institute.
[ ] Yes, include me on the Norman Institute's mailing list.

$\mathcal{n}_{\ell}$ norman institute

(promotional and distribution agent for Just Tell the Truth)

Just Tell the Truth is about the thousands of gay men who enter heterosexual marriages, father children, and remain quietly in the closet until they voluntarily disclose their true gender orientation. Its purpose is to provide clear, concise answers to the questions families ask when gay married men come out. In a broader sense, however, this book should prove helpful to anyone seeking to understand the journey toward orientational authenticity.

Orders may be placed for next day shipping by:
Calling our office at (816) 960-7200
Or, by filling out the attached order form and returning it to:

Norman Institute Bookstore
P.O. Box 45600
Kansas City, Missouri 64171

- -

Order Form - *Just Tell the Truth*

Name: _____

Address: _____

City: _____ State: _____ Zip: _____

Phone: (____)_____ (Necessary only with credit card orders)

Please send _____ book(s) @ $15.95 each
(Handling charge included)   = _____

All orders shipped Priority Mail (1 to 4 day delivery):
Add $3.00 for 1-4 books; or $6.00 for 5-8 books   + _____
(For discounts and shipping rates on quantity orders, call 816-960-7200)

ORDER TOTAL: $ _____

Payment Method: [ ] Money Order   [ ] Visa   [ ] Mastercard   [ ] Check

Credit Card Number: _____

Expiration Date: _____ Signature: _____

[ ] Please send me information about the Norman Institute.
[ ] Yes, include me on the Norman Institute's mailing list.